Guide to Psychic Protection

Guide to Psychic Protection

Rosemary Ellen Guiley

Visionary Living Publishing/Visionary Living, Inc.
New Milford, Connecticut

Guide to Psychic Protection

By Rosemary Ellen Guiley

Copyright Rosemary Ellen Guiley, 2018

All rights reserved.
No part of this book may be reproduced in any form or used without permission.

Front cover design by April Slaughter
Back cover and interior design by Leslie McAllister
Original drawings by John Weaver

ISBN: 978-1-942157-27-4 (pbk)
ISBN: 978-1-942157-28-1 (epub)

Published by Visionary Living Publishing/Visionary Living, Inc.
New Milford, Connecticut
www.visionarylivingpublishing.com

Author's Note

Much of my fieldwork in the paranormal has involved dealing with dark and negative energy and forces: spirit attachments, problem hauntings, hostile entities and even toxic people. I am often asked what I do to protect myself prior to exposure to negative conditions, and what I do if I am affected by negativity.

Psychic hazards extend far beyond paranormal activities to every aspect of life – you can run into negativity anywhere: at work, out in public and even at home.

People have different tolerances and boundaries; what greatly disturbs one person will barely ruffle another. It's important to know your own boundaries and how to strengthen them.

Psychic protection is not something that is flipped on and off like a switch. Protection should always be around you, and it is built up by knowledge, awareness and sound practices. If you do your spiritual homework on an ongoing basis, you will fortify a tremendous field of protection around you that you will carry all the time.

This basic guide covers the most common types of psychic attack and psychic vampirism from both human and nonhuman sources and provides a wealth of remedies and defenses.

I would like to thank John Weaver for his original drawings, and Kelly Weaver for her clairvoyant impressions of auras.

Table of Contents

Author's Note	v
1. Psychic Attack and Psychic Vampirism	1
2. Sources of Psychic Attack and Psychic Vampirism	15
3. The Importance of the Aura	39
4. Aura Defenses	57
5. Calling on Spiritual Forces	67
6. Malevolent Stares	85
7. Dream and Sleep Invasion	95
8. Amulets	109
9. More Remedial Measures	127
Appendix: A Home Blessing	133
About the Author	137
Further Reading	139

Chapter 1

Psychic Attack and Psychic Vampirism

Have you ever spent time with a person who left you feeling strangely limp and drained of energy? Have you had to work with someone who was always leveling intense stares at you? Have you been to a place where, as soon as you walked in, the very "atmosphere" made you feel uncomfortable or even ill? And perhaps that feeling went home with you?

Most of us have had at least a few episodes of such experiences. Fortunately, in most cases, the effects soon pass. Sometimes, however, the effects not only linger but escalate and take a serious toll on overall health and well-being.

If you have had such experiences, you may have encountered psychic attack, an often subtle and sometimes deliberate means of weakening your vital life force. Psychic attack is also called psychic vampirism. Psychic attack can be perpetrated by people who know techniques for doing so, and by people who are unwitting energy drainers. It also comes from hostile and malevolent entities. If you encounter psychic attack, it is more likely to come from people than spirits or entities.

Psychic attack affects currents and fields of energy. We live in a cosmic sea of energy exchanges. We take in a vital life force that permeates everything in existence, and powers life itself and our health. We put out streams of energy in return. We have natural barriers against negative forces, but under some conditions those barriers can be breached – and without us even realizing it.

The need for psychic protection is not limited to warding off targeted psychic attacks. Every day, we encounter hostile and aggressive people and situations, all of which can have a negative impact on our vitality. Psychic protection shields us from unwanted negativity, deflecting it before it has a chance to impact us.

The experiences of Dion Fortune

For classic examples of psychic attack, we can turn to the English occultist Dion Fortune (1891-1946), who became one of the leading experts on the subject. Her expertise remains unrivaled today.

DION FORTUNE

Psychic Self-Defense

The Classic Instruction Manual for Protecting
Yourself Against Paranormal Attack

'we live in the midst of invisible forces'

She was born Violet Mary Firth. "Dion Fortune" was her pen name, taken from her magical motto, *Deo Non Fortuna* ("By God, not chance").

Fortune became an expert on psychic attack through her own experience, which she described in her book *Psychic Self-Defense* (1930). She had her first encounter with psychic attack as a young woman of 20. She took a job working for a woman who had extensive occult knowledge she had learned during a residency in India. The woman controlled her staff with techniques of mind power, and some of her employees suffered mysterious breakdowns.

Fortune herself became the object of mind manipulation when her boss wanted her to give testimony in a lawsuit. The testimony contradicted Fortune's direct knowledge of the events surrounding the suit, and she resisted. But after spending time in the presence of her boss, who gave her an intense gaze and directed her in what to say, Fortune became so dazed and exhausted she was forced to retire to bed, where she slept for 15 straight hours. During a second session with her boss, she found herself agreeing to baseless charges. This session also was followed by extreme exhaustion and a dead sleep.

When Fortune then decided to terminate her employment, her boss used the same technique to try to break her will. "You are incompetent, and you know it. You have no self-confidence and you have got to admit it," the woman said. Fortune denied this. Her boss kept up this litany for four hours. "I entered her room at ten o'clock, and I left it at two," Fortune wrote years later. "She must have said these two phrases several hundreds of times. I entered it a strong and healthy girl. I left it a mental and physical wreck and was ill for three years."

Fortune's experience caused her to research occultism to determine what had happened to her, and how she could have defended herself against it. "My body was like an electric battery that had been completely discharged," she said. "It took a long time to charge up again, and every time it was used before charging was completed, it ran down again rapidly. For a long time, I had no reserves of energy, and after the least exertion would fall into a dead sleep at any hour of the day."

Her research led her to conclude that damage had been sustained by her etheric double (also called the "etheric template"), a layer of the aura that channels the universal life force to the body for physical health, and for our personality and self-expression. Fortune believed that the damage to her etheric double, caused by this woman, created a leak in her life force. Thus, she suffered profound exhaustion and mental fatigue.

Fortune furthered her knowledge by joining the ranks of leading occultists. She became a member of the Stella Matutina, an outer order of the esteemed Hermetic Order of the Golden Dawn. The Golden Dawn was formed in the late 19th century in London as an esoteric order and soon became a magical order. Its members included many of the most skilled occultists of the day. After a period of time in the Golden Dawn, Fortune left and formed her own order, which became the Society of the Inner Light.

Fortune was gifted psychically and mediumistically and had a great talent for the magical arts. She witnessed bizarre phenomena and participated in psychic feuds, fending off psychic attacks in the name of the Masters of the Great White Lodge. As she wrote later, she "kept the occult vigil when one dare not sleep while the sun is below the horizon; and hung on desperately, matching my staying-power against the attack until the moon-tides changed and the force of the onslaught blew itself out." She worked as a psychiatrist and attributed many of the symptoms in cases she saw to psychic attacks.

Fortune's work and experiences gained her expert knowledge of how psychic attacks occur, their symptoms in unsuspecting victims, and how the attacks can be warded off or nullified. "I am of the opinion that psychic attacks are far commoner than is generally realized, even by occultists themselves," she said.

The purposes of psychic attack are to weaken, debilitate and destroy; to bend the will of the victim; or to draw off life force energy that is used by the attacker. In all cases, the victim ultimately is psychically vampirized due to a loss of life force. Exhaustion sets in, and in extreme cases, the victim may fall seriously ill.

Fortune believed herself to be psychically attacked numerous times. In one case, she awoke one morning with dried blood on her pillow from a small puncture behind the angle of the jaw. She attributed the puncture to an attack by a girl who was a psychic vampire. Others in the girl's proximity reported getting the same puncture marks and blood spots.

Fortune's help was sought by many who feared they were victims of occult attack. One case was that of a Mr. C. and his two wives who were victimized by a Miss X. As a young girl, Miss X had been engaged to a man who, soon after the engagement was announced, developed consumption and died of a violent hemorrhage. A few years later, she became engaged again and the second fiancé also developed consumption. Although he, too, hemorrhaged, his illness lingered, and he lived as an invalid for years. During his illness, Miss X took a house, moved him in and installed an aunt as chaperone. The aunt soon developed listlessness and for days at a stretch would lie unconscious. However, no cause of her illness could be found.

While her fiancé and aunt were ill, Miss X entertained herself by visiting Mr. and Mrs. C. She became infatuated with Mr. C., but her attentions went unrequited. Mrs. C. soon died of uterine cancer. Much to the chagrin of Miss X, Mr. C. married another woman. The health of the second Mrs. C. soon declined. She suffered nightmares, epileptic-like fits, weakness and fatigue. Eventually she was diagnosed as having uterine cancer. She, too, died.

At about the same time, Miss X's aunt and second fiancé also succumbed. Miss X suffered a mental breakdown and was admitted to a nursing home in the country. In all likelihood, Fortune concluded, her vampirism finally turned on herself.

Most cases of psychic attack are not so extreme, but this one illustrates the potential danger involved.

Fortune's book *Psychic Self-Defense* is still in print today and is considered one of the best resources on psychic attack.

"The Parasite"

Today Sir Arthur Conan Doyle (1859-1930) is best-known for his Sherlock Holmes mysteries, but his personal interests spread deeply into the paranormal and occult. He was active in psychical research of mediumship, survival after death, and Spiritualism. He also knew a great deal about psychic attack.

In 1894, long before his contemporary, Dion Fortune, had her devastating experience with her superior at work, Doyle wrote a novelette or short story, "The Parasite," describing in chilling detail the predatory tactics that Fortune would soon encounter. It was initially published in *Harper's Weekly*, and eventually went on to be adapted into a film in 1997.

Doyle offers no information in any introductory remarks as to his motives for writing the story. Did he learn about psychic attack from his occult-educated peers, and thought it would make a great story? Or was he a victim of psychic attack himself?

The psychic vampire in Doyle's story is Miss Penelosa, a crippled old maid who becomes obsessed with a much younger college professor named Austin Gilroy, who does not believe in the occult. His lack of belief and knowledge will soon be to his peril.

Miss Penelosa is deceptive in appearance – she certainly does not look like someone who could destroy a person's life. She is a small and frail creature "with a pale, peaky face, an insignificant presence and retiring manner." She requires a crutch to walk about. This appearance turns out to be misleading, to the destruction of Gilroy.

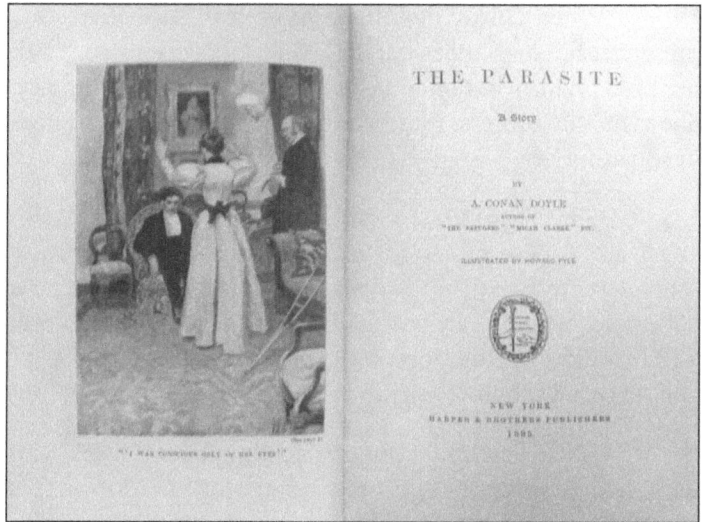

"The Parasite" frontispiece in Harper's Weekly *magazine.*

Miss Penelosa's vampiric powers are evidenced in her remarkable eyes. She first attacks Gilroy's fianceé, Agatha, mesmerizing her. Then she saps the professor's vitality, making him waste away and acquire dark, sunken eyes. To his horror, he realizes that he has fallen under her influence, and that she is a "monster parasite" who "creeps into my form as the hermit crab creeps into the whelk's shell." He tries to resist, but whenever he is in her presence he becomes weaker still.

Gilroy shuts himself up in his bedroom and tosses the key out the window into the garden. He experiences some relief, but then he learns that Miss Penelosa has been ill at the same time, and her powers weaken whenever she is ill. He remains sequestered, but when she regains her strength and powers, he is irresistibly pulled out.

When Gilroy next finds himself in Miss Penelosa's presence, he denounces her in a fury. This seems to break her hold on him, but once again the effect is only temporary. She visits the professor and warns him of the consequences in spurning her.

Gilroy's continued loathing incites Miss Penelosa to anger and a determination to destroy him. She persecutes him mercilessly. Gilroy is driven to confide his woes to a colleague, who prescribes traditional remedies of chloral and bromide. Gilroy does not believe these will help him, and he throws them in a gutter.

Miss Penelosa foments gossip about Gilroy and uses her powers to ruin his concentration during his lectures, causing him to babble nonsense. He becomes a laughingstock and is suspended from his position.

Alone and in despair, Gilroy knows that no one will believe the truth about what has happened to him. He descends into madness, robs a bank, assaults a friend and nearly mutilates the face of Agatha. His misery ends only when Miss Penelosa suddenly dies.

"The Parasite" is a dark story, for the protagonist has no effective defense against the vampire, who ensnares him in a spider-like way. His only relief comes through her death due to outside circumstances.

Doyle went for tragedy in "The Parasite," but psychic attack need not end that way. Just as Fortune found her way out of dire circumstances, so do others. The best approach to psychic attack is prevention and defense, and knowledgeable responses if defenses are breached.

Symptoms of psychic attack and psychic vampirism

Symptoms of an attack are varied and include unexplained behavior; disturbed dreams and violent nightmares; bedroom visitations by dark entities; repulsive smells; exhaustion; dizziness; mental confusion and breakdown; foreign and alien thoughts, especially of an unpleasant or violent nature; unexplained and unresolved illness; the outbreak of poltergeist phenomena in the home; unexplained bruises, cuts or small marks resembling pricks or bites; and mental or physical possession.

Not every case of psychic attack involves all or even most of these symptoms. Some of them are related to natural causes, and so one should not automatically assume psychic attack, but rule out natural explanations first.

Vulnerable circumstances

Psychic attack can be carried out around the clock. However, we have windows of greater vulnerability. As mentioned, sleeping is a vulnerable state. During the night, we are most vulnerable between 3 and 5 AM, when the life force currents are lower. It is no accident that many victims say they woke up to a bedroom visitation at around 3 AM.

Similarly, we are at an energy low point between 2 and 4 PM during the day. This is often a time when people feel drowsy and unfocused.

The waning and dark moon phases are vulnerable times as well, when the lunar forces on the tides of life are lower. The moon regulates the tides of the oceans, and in occultism also regulates the flow of the life force in the body, including blood and vital fluids. Thus, the waxing moon brings increased strength and vitality and the waning moon brings an ebb of energy. This is what Fortune referred to when she described how, in her psychic attack defense, she "hung on desperately, matching my staying-power against the attack until the moon-tides changed…"

Fortune identified four major conditions of vulnerability:

- *Being in a place where occult forces are concentrated.* Examples are haunted places polluted by negative energy and presences, such as old prisons, sanitoriums and asylums, and places where considerable ritual activity has been carried out.

- *Encountering people who are adept at handling occult forces.* Some of them are opportunists who will take advantage of others.

- *Dabbling in the occult and getting out of one's depth.* The popularity of ghost investigating has drawn many people into experimenting with spirit summoning without having the proper background, knowledge or training.

- *Falling victim to certain pathological conditions.* Poor health on any level – physical, mental, emotional or spiritual – weakens the vital life force and the aura boundary that surrounds the body.

Chapter 2

Sources of Psychic Attack and Psychic Vampirism

Most people will never experience the extreme levels of psychic attack described and experienced by Dion Fortune. Her boss, as she noted, was skilled in occult techniques. After Fortune became involved in the magical community, the occult battles she engaged in on the astral plane were fought by skilled adepts. Psychic attack was carried out by thoughtform and by engaging the help of malevolent entities.

There are other sources of deliberate and unwitting attack that we are more likely to encounter. Most of the remedies for them are dealt with in the subsequent chapters. Some are given in this chapter.

Toxic people

Toxic people are individuals who harbor resentment, anger and envy. They spew out negative energy, and others around them may be impacted by it, depending upon their sensitivity and vulnerability. Sometimes their hostility is deliberately directed at an individual: someone they dislike, want to control or see as a rival. Some of them may know enough about hypnosis or the projection of mental energy to strike out deliberately against a person; for example, to try to make them feel weak, disempowered or undesirable.

The energy coming off toxic people can boomerang around public places. When it is concentrated, directed and ongoing, such as in personal relationships and workplace environments, it can become a serious problem.

Curses

Human beings have leveled curses against one another since ancient times. As Plato noted in his *Republic*, "If anyone wishes to injure an enemy, for a small fee they [sorcerers] will bring harm on good or bad alike, binding the gods to serve their purposes by spells and curses." The Romans consulted professional cursers to act out against their rivals and enemies, even in sporting events. The curses were written and invoked the aid of spirits and the gods to carry them out.

Most curses are a form of psychic attack intended to bring misfortune, illness, harm or even death to a victim. They are "laid" or "thrown" primarily for revenge and power. Some curses are for protection of homes, treasures, tombs and gravesites – violators will suffer. A curse can take effect quickly or may be dormant for years. Curses have been laid upon families, plaguing them for generations.

Every culture today has beliefs in, and techniques for, cursing. People throw curses themselves, or they engage the services of someone skilled in the occult and magical arts. Most curses are of a highly personal nature, and usually revolve around love rivalries, spurned love, money issues and personal revenge.

The ancients wrote their curses and invoked supernatural help in carrying them out. Other methods of cursing are to use substitutes for the victim, such as a waxen image, poppet (small doll) or photograph. Whatever is done to the substitute supposedly will be done to and felt by the victim.

The cursed gift is a frequent method of delivering psychic attack. Any object can be imbued with a curse – jewelry, clothing, paintings, furniture, accessories, personal items and so on, just as objects can be imbued with healing and protective energy. In our book *Haunted by the Things You Love* (2014), John Zaffis and I document cases of cursed objects that wreaked havoc with the victims. In several cases, the object was a gift from a spurned lover who pretended to make amends but really sought to break up a new relationship or a marriage. The victims experienced nightmares, disturbing poltergeist phenomena, deteriorating health, and stress with their spouses or partners.

The most common form of cursing, and the one most likely to be experienced in everyday life, is "ill-wishing." It involves the harboring of resentment, anger, jealousy and other negative energy against a person, combined with wishing that bad things will happen to them. Workplace competition and family rivalries can generate quite a bit of ill-wishing.

People engage in ill-wishing all the time. Much of it never impacts the target because it is intermittent and not focused. However, a steady stream of ill-wishing can be debilitating, if nothing more than to cause discomfort in another person. Toxic people are likely to engage in ill-wishing a great deal, even if they do not realize exactly what they are doing. They are unhappy with themselves and their lives and blame others for it. Ill-wishing can be deflected and neutralized with the remedies offered in this book.

If you suspect you have been given a cursed object, do not leave it in your home or work environment but remove it immediately. Invoke prayers and spiritual help to neutralize the curse and dispose of the object by wrapping it and burying it in earth or deep water, or by throwing it away. Do not burn an object, for the sudden destruction may cause an expulsion of an occupying spirit, which will immediately seek attachment to something – or someone – else.

Formal cursing, in which a skilled person has been engaged to throw a curse with the help of low-level spirits, usually requires getting the help of someone equally skilled who knows how to break or nullify it.

Unwitting "energy vampires"

Not all cases of psychic vampirism are perpetrated by a calculating and malevolent individual. Some people are

Sources of Psychic Attack and Psychic Vampirism

unwitting energy vampires. We've all encountered individuals from time to time who leave us inexplicably wrung out and tired. They go spinning along like little psychic tornadoes, sucking up everyone in their paths and tossing them out drained and limp. Quite often it's impossible to pinpoint exactly what it is about such persons that makes being in their presence so exhausting. It's rarely anything specific they do or say. These unwitting energy vampires often are bright and cheerful people. They have boundless energy – they have borrowed *yours*.

Dr. Edward C. Berridge, a homeopathic physician who was a skilled adept in the Hermetic Order of the Golden Dawn in England, documented many cases of psychic vampirism.

In one case, Berridge was repeatedly visited by an elderly man of "exhausted nervous vitality" who always made Berridge feel exhausted. It occurred to him that the old man was preying upon him – he was a toxic person and a psychic vampire, but an unwitting one.

"I don't suppose he was at all externally conscious that he possessed a vampire nature, for he was a benevolent, kind-hearted man, who would have shrunk in horror from such a suggestion," Berridge wrote. However, he believed the old man was in other respects an intentional vampire, for he admitted to wanting to marry a much younger woman in the hopes of revitalizing himself.

Psychic vampires are not things of the past or relegated to magical circles. They exist everywhere. A Chicago paranormal researcher and acquaintance of mine described such an energy vampire:

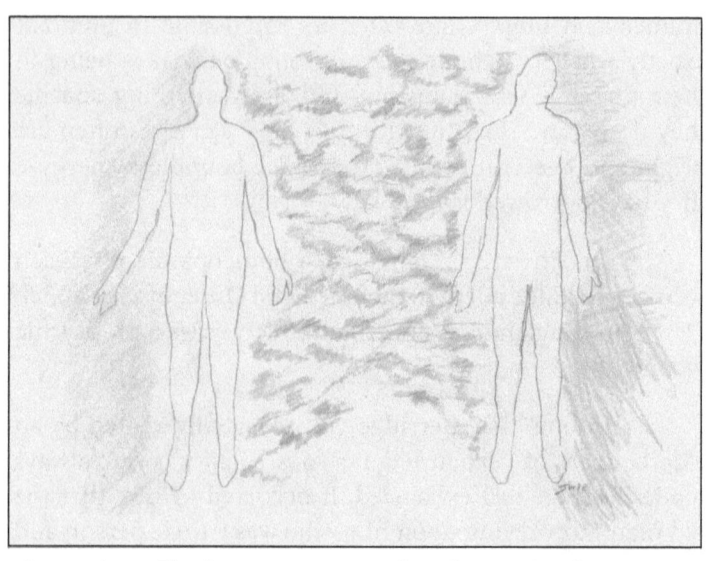

Interactions with others generate a mingling of energy. Psychic vampires can draw someone else's energy to them. Credit: John Weaver.

> *I knew an individual who was part of a group of friends I was in. The rest of us determined that there was something definitely different about him in that he had the ability to leech off other people's energy. It wasn't obvious at first – it took a while to understand. It was nothing blatant that he did. His physical activity actually seemed rather low. Yet half a dozen people or more expressed the opinion that he was able to drain off energy. There was something about him that made it exhausting to be in the same room with him. He had this unwarranted intensity about him at all times.*
>
> *Everything to him was an earthshaking ordeal. Not that he became overwrought, but he had this indefinable straining forward at all times. The simplest conversation would be pursued with this kind of grim and plodding charge. It's hard to put into words because I've never since met anyone like him. After a fifteen-minute conversation with him, I would feel like going to bed exhausted. We took a dislike to him. I don't think he was aware of his effect and seemed baffled by others keeping their distance.*

I too have known individuals like this. One was a woman acquaintance who carried an intensity about her all the time. Everything that happened in her life, including the most trivial and mundane event, was treated at a crisis energy level that she wanted others to share. Spending time with her drained me.

Another woman, whom I met in writers' circles in New York City, had the uncanny ability to vacuum energy from people. Her conversation and mannerisms were ordinary, but when I was around her and engaged in conversation, I always felt she was somehow pulling energy out of me at the same time. I do not think she was ever aware of what she was doing – but she was always full of energy herself.

The "unwitting energy vampire" usually has no intention to harm others. Nonetheless, there are ways to protect yourself from this kind of energy invasion.

Hostile entities

In some cases, dark entities are responsible for psychic attack and vampirism. These include, but are not limited to, demons, Djinn, elementals, hostile spirits and beings, and shadow people.

The proliferation of paranormal reality shows in which people are harassed by demonic and violent entities may give some viewers the impression that this is a widespread hazard. However, many people will never encounter hostile nonhuman entities and spirits.

Hostile entities can occupy haunted locations, including homes, and act out against whoever lives or stays there. In such cases, the most vulnerable person will be the first to experience unpleasant phenomena and psychic attack. The longer the attack goes on, the more likely others in the house or environment will experience the effects as well. Some people get help to expel the hostile entities; in other cases, the entities resist all expulsion attempts, and the only solution is to leave the location. In a small number of cases, entities attach to people and follow them.

Hostile entities also can be drawn to people by the wrong kinds of spirit activity, such as summoning and rituals intended to invoke certain spirits. Sometimes individuals who play at summoning in hopes of getting a dangerous thrill wind up getting more than they bargained for.

Hostile entity attacks do not occur without a cause, however, and the cause must be determined before the most appropriate remedies can be applied.

Djinn

The Djinn are a race of intelligent beings older than humans that share the planet with us. They have the ability to shapeshift and be physical or nonphysical, and to cross from their parallel world into ours. "Djinn" is Arabic for "Hidden Ones." Most of the knowledge of Djinn originates in the Middle East, but the Djinn – known to Westerners as genies – are everywhere.

Some Djinn like to meddle in the affairs of humans, and some are hostile and even malevolent. If crossed by humans, they may act out in psychic attacks. They can be summoned via sorcery to attack people as well.

In the West, Djinn are often mistaken for demons because their behavior is similar, and they can assume demonic-like forms. There are exorcisms and banishments for Djinn. In cases of negative hauntings where I have suspected or identified the presence of Djinn, I have recommended consultation with Djinn experts, most of whom can be found in Muslim communities.

Spirit board entities

People love to play with spirit boards like the Ouija, a device for communicating with the spirit realm. People who are familiar with my work know that I consider the spirit board to be a neutral device – using one is not going to automatically call in a negative spirit. Hollywood presents a much different picture, and films and television shows are full of "true" stories of Ouija activity gone bad.

Most people will never have a problem with a spirit board. There exists the potential, however, that a hostile entity will be drawn to a board session, scare people – and not leave. The reasons why malevolent spirits drop in are many, and often have to do with the players themselves and the circumstances under which they are using the board. Regardless of the cause, once you've got a nasty presence that won't go away after the session is ended opens the door to psychic attack.

Victims can experience the full range of symptoms described earlier. In my book with Darren Evans, *The Zozo Phenomenon* (2016), we document terrifying experiences with an entity that usually calls itself Zozo. Some of the victims never heard of Zozo until it spelled its name out on a board and then went crazy on the players.

When low-level entities like Zozo get a foot in the door, they can attach to a spirit board, an environment, or a person. Remedies include getting rid of or destroying the board and cleansing the environment as prescribed in this book. As mentioned earlier in regards to cursed objects, do not burn a board, but wrap it up and dispose of it by burial in earth or deep water, or in trash. In cases of personal attachment, professional help may be needed to dislodge the entity and send it away.

Some spirit board predators are more interested in pranking (silly messages, dire warnings and poltergeist effects), and do not cause serious trouble. In many cases, they go away when forcefully ordered to do so, or they are put out of business when a board session is closed. Environmental cleansings are advisable.

Shadow people

Shadow people are dark entities, usually in the shape of humans, who make bedroom visits to terrify people. Sometimes just their manifestation at the foot of a bed or in the doorway will psychically vampirize the victim; sometimes they assault the victim physically by grabbing them, leaping upon them, or pressing down on them with a suffocating or choking effect.

They can appear during the day as well and cause haunting phenomena, such as black blobs seen moving through hallways or manifesting in rooms, and poltergeist effects.

A shadow person makes a terrifying bedroom visit. Credit: John Weaver.

The most common form taken by shadow people is a completely black silhouette of a tall man, six to seven feet in height, often wearing a coat or cloak, and sometimes a hat or hood. They are described as "blacker than black," standing out against the darkness. They appear to have solid mass, yet they can turn into mist or smoke and vanish in an instant.

I have studied shadow people for years, documenting their characteristics and the circumstances under which they manifest. I have related them to the Djinn, a type of supernatural being that likes to pester people; they also have demonic characteristics. Their purpose seems to be to vampirize the life force out of people. When they appear, the victim is immediately frightened, and an adrenalin rush sets in. I believe the shadow people draw off this energy for their own purposes.

Shadow people have been documented throughout history, though the term "shadow people" is of recent origin. In the past, they have been described as dark ghosts, demons and black phantom monks and nuns. Even earlier descriptions of the Devil as "the Black Man" or "the Man in Black" could have been descriptions of shadow people.

Shadow people attack humans for many reasons. Some are attached to land, and so any dwelling or structure built on top of the land will be occupied by them, and they will act out against the human occupants. Others find ways to attach to people when their auras are weakened, such as through illness or stress. Some have generational links, following family members from age to age. These cases are often related to spirit summoning gone wrong in the past.

In my research on shadow people, I found that certain people who were under emotional stress and chaos seemed to attract these beings. For example, individuals undergoing severe stress and trauma experienced a spate of shadow people visits, which stopped when the individual regained equilibrium. Certainly not everyone undergoing stress will experience shadow people, however.

Elementals

Elementals are beings created from the four elements of nature. They are evoked in magical rites. Natural elementals are sometimes involved in haunting phenomena.

The classes of elemental spirits and their elements are:

- Earth: Gnomes or pygmies
- Water: Undines or nymphs
- Fire: Salamanders
- Air: Sylphs

According to the Swiss alchemist Paracelsus (1493-1541), all elementals have human form and can mix with humans, yet they have no relationship to humans and are not descended from Adam and Eve. They are not spirits per se, but are made in the image of man, with flesh, bones and blood. However, they are higher than man, for they are of both the physical and spirit worlds. They are mortal. They live according to instinct and reason.

Elementals can enter the human world, but humans cannot enter the realms of the elementals, because the physical body is too coarse. Some elementals are generous to humans, helping them in tasks and chores and bestowing gifts, such as treasures, upon them. Others are hostile and create haunting phenomena and other problems.

Elemental spirits can attach to people and can be commanded via ritual.

Dr. Edward C. Berridge, mentioned earlier, also had experiences with energy-draining elementals. In one of his cases, a woman sought his help concerning her failing health. She had pursued spiritual development and had become "passively mediumistic," that is, open to the influences of the spirit realm. Evidently, she had weaknesses in her natural barriers, for she became susceptible to the draining influence of low-level entities.

Berridge did some mesmeric hand passes over her to infuse her with life force energy, and he placed an envelope of the universal life force (discussed in the next chapter) around her as a protective layer to shut out the negative entities.

The woman's health and strength improved, and her mediumistic experiences stopped. She missed them, and soon reopened herself mediumistically. She went into another health decline. After a lingering illness, she died.

Berridge said he was attacked by an attached elemental that he believed turned on him when he shut it off from the woman. He wrote:

> *I had not yet been initiated into the G.D. [Golden Dawn] then, or I should have*

afterwards used [a ritual] for my own protection. About two weeks after, I had a vivid dream that I was endeavoring to evoke an elemental, which attacked me, causing a sudden choking in the throat, and an electric shock in the body. The dream had an astrological meaning; and at the same time I believe it had a physical basis and that the same vampirizing spirit which had been preying on its victim, determined to attack me, in revenge for having thwarted its designs.

Note: Opening up mediumistically does not automatically result in negative entity attachment. There were other factors in the woman's health and life that enabled the elemental attachment to take place.

Elementaries

Elementaries are artificial beings similar to thoughtforms (see below). Paracelsus distinguished elementaries from elementals. Elementaries are not part of the natural order, he said, but are evil beings created in the invisible realms by excesses of human thought and emotion, corruption of character, degeneration of faculties and misuse of powers.

Elementaries are dependent upon humans for existence and initially for survival. If they are nourished enough by human negativity, they gain an independence, and can turn on their creators, draining them of their life force and vitality. Examples of elementaries are vampiric entities and sexual predators such as the incubus and succubus. If they attach to people like parasites, they can exacerbate mental disorders such as obsession, and negative physical actions such as anger, aggression and corruption. They can also contribute to physical disease.

Fear, depression, self-pity and feelings of victimization can open the door for attachment of elementaries, Paracelsus said. Recovery is accomplished through a reversal of thoughts and emotions to the positive, which literally starves the elementaries and forces them away.

Franz Bardon (1909-1958), one of the great occultists of the 20th century, defined elementaries as astral beings created out of an element by a skilled person or adept. The creator imbues the elementary with some of his or her own consciousness, and the elementary feeds off of that energy as long as it is active. The creator gives the elementary a name, assigns it tasks, and sets a finite lifespan for it. When the tasks are completed, the elementary ideally dissolves back into the astral matrix.

However, elementaries are intelligent, and if they are not strictly controlled by their creator, they will gain independence and go out of control.

Thoughtforms

A thoughtform is a nonphysical entity or object created by thought that exists in the mental plane or the astral plane.

We create thoughtforms all the time. For example, whenever you set your intention on a goal, you create a thoughtform that attracts what you are seeking. If the intention is strong and sustained, and accompanied by action and perseverance, you reach your goal. You also create a thoughtform when you sustain anger or resentment, or constantly criticize yourself as a "victim."

Thoughtforms are used in magic and the casting of spells for many purposes, positive and negative, including psychic attack.

Esoteric philosophy holds that thoughts produce two effects: a radiating vibration and a floating, colored form. The lifespan and endurance of a thoughtform depends on the nature and intensity of the thought. Most thoughtforms dissipate unless they are continually energized. They are invisible to most people but can be perceived clairvoyantly.

Annie Besant and Charles W. Leadbeater, Theosophists and clairvoyants, said thoughtforms are four-dimensional in nature, and therefore are difficult to describe in three-dimensional terms.

Thoughts which are low in nature, such as anger, hate, lust and greed, create thoughtforms that are dense in color and form. Thoughts of a more spiritual nature generate forms that have greater purity, clarity and refinement. Besant and Leadbeater said that well-sustained devotion might appear as a flower with upward curving petals like azure flames, and devotional aspiration as a blue cone with the apex pointing upward to the higher planes.

On the opposite end, explosive anger appears as a splash of red or orange, and sustained anger as a sharp, red stiletto. Jealousy might appear as a brown snake.

The clairvoyant impressions of thoughtforms are not uniform or constant, but relevant to the percipient and the situation. In general, positive and spiritual thoughtforms have pleasing forms and colors, while negative thoughtforms have unpleasant and repulsive features.

Thoughtforms build up in a person's energy field or aura, creating and influencing behavior and characteristics. Negative thoughts weaken a person, even facilitating the onset of illness or spirit attachment, while positive and loving thoughts act as a protective, energizing shield.

According to Besant and Leadbeater, selfish thought moves in a curve, eventually coming back on itself (and the person) and expending itself on its own level. Those who send out negativity run a high risk of getting it back on themselves.

On the other hand, unselfish thought moves outward in an open curve, expanding as it goes. It is capable of piercing higher spiritual dimensions and thus becomes a channel through which higher planes pour themselves into lower planes. This is how prayer functions.

Thoughtforms called "artificial elementals" are created by ritual to perform tasks and errands, and to be directed at individuals to protect, heal or harm. To have an effect, thoughtforms must be able to latch on to similar vibrations in the aura of the recipient. Thus, someone whose aura is weakened with negativity might be vulnerable to a negative thoughtform or elemental. If the elemental is unable to attach, it boomerangs back to the sender.

The duration and strength of a thoughtform depend on the strength and clarity of the original thought. Some thoughtforms have the capability to assume their own energy and appear to be intelligent and independent. Equally intense thought can disperse them, or, they can simply disintegrate when their purpose is finished. Some may last years. In magical practice it is customary to charge a thoughtform with a finite life span.

Thoughtforms that are not dispersed, as well as some powerful thoughtforms, can go out of control. They wander about looking for energy sources and attach themselves to people like vampiric entities. Or, they can turn on their creators, as in the case of Alexandra David-Neel, an Englishwoman who became famous in the early 20th century for her bold explorations of Tibet.

David-Neel mastered the Tibetan technique for creating a thoughtform called a *tulpa*. She intended it to have the form of a lama who would be "short and fat, of an innocent and jolly type." She spent several months performing the ritual, and at last a phantom monk appeared. It assumed a life-like form and existed like a guest in David-Neel's apartment.

The *tulpa* tagged along with her as she went on a tour. Then it began to change. She wrote, "The fat, chubby-cheeked fellow grew leaner, his face assumed a vaguely mocking, sly, malignant look. He became more troublesome and bold. In brief, he escaped my control." The *tulpa* began touching her and rubbing up against her. Others began to see him, but he did not respond to anyone's conversation.

Alexandra David-Neel

David-Neel attempted to dissolve the *tulpa*, but it had gained so much power that it resisted her efforts. It took her six months to eliminate him. The entire episode upset her, and she termed it "very bad luck."

Dion Fortune also had an unhappy episode with a thoughtform she created herself: a menacing wolf form that arose out of her own internalized anger and resentment against someone who had tried to do her harm.

The wolf thoughtform appeared in her bedroom at night, and she knew immediately that it might go beyond her control unless she took swift action. After consulting one of her magical superiors, she reabsorbed the energy and released her desire for revenge. The experience was a valuable lesson in how we can affect ourselves through our own negativity.

One of the severest self-generated thoughtform psychic attacks on record is the "Thornton Heath Poltergeist" case in England in 1938. It was labeled a poltergeist case because of the outbreak of poltergeist phenomena that first attracted the attention of investigators and the media. The case was documented by Nandor Fodor, a respected psychical researcher.

The focal point was Pat Forbes, who lived with her husband at Thornton Heath. The poltergeist activity started suddenly. Objects flew about the house, dropped from ceilings and materialized from thin air. Glasses shattered. Pungent smells of violets and rotting flesh permeated the air. The phenomena escalated in frequency and strangeness until Mrs. Forbes reported the horror of being visited and attacked by an invisible vampire at night.

She reported an unpleasant weight like a cold human body pressing upon her in bed. In the morning, she awakened feeling limp and drained. There were tiny puncture marks on her neck. Fodor said her experiences "read like a page from Bram Stoker's *Dracula*."

After a lengthy investigation, Fodor discovered that Mrs. Forbes had experienced a traumatic childhood involving rape, severe illness and psychic experiences of hauntings by ghosts. In her twenties she suffered from hysterical blindness, coma, a debilitating kidney ailment, breast cancer and alienation from her husband at the time. She expressed a bizarre attraction to graveyards. All these things had been repressed.

Fodor did not label the invisible "vampire" as a thoughtform, but the characteristics of the case have the hallmarks of one that is generated and projected from within. Unfortunately, he was not allowed to conclude his investigation and see Mrs. Forbes to a resolution. His diagnosis of the case as a sexual neurosis outraged the Council of the International Institute for Psychical Research, under whose auspices he was working, and he was dismissed from his post as research officer for the Institute. Hopefully, Mrs. Forbes received the therapy she needed.

Earthbound spirits

Some people do not make a transition to the afterlife upon death but remain earthbound in a twilight in which they are neither here nor there. They become earthbound for a variety of reasons: they may not know they are dead, due to the sudden circumstances of their passing; they may fear going into the afterlife; or they have unfinished business on earth, to which they have a strong emotional attachment.

Earthbounds are more lost than hostile. They linger in places and appear to others as ghosts. They may or may not be able to communicate. Sometimes they are looking for help.

Earthbounds are attracted to the auras and spiritual lights of the living, and can attach themselves to auras, which has a draining effect.

Hostile earthbounds may have grudges or revenge scores they are trying to settle, and some are capable of causing significant disturbances and energy drains.

Some earthbounds eventually find their way to the afterlife, while others need help from individuals skilled in spirit releasement.

Chapter 3

The Importance of the Aura

Everyone is born with a natural barrier against negativity. This barrier is the aura, an envelope of energy that surrounds the body and protects physical, mental, emotional and spiritual well-being. The aura is composed of the vital universal life force of the cosmos that emanates from the Source of All-Being. The universal life force is called by various names, including *chi* and *prana*.

When the aura is strong and healthy, it provides an effective natural barrier against unwanted forces and energies; it is like your body's immune system that automatically repels any invaders. The aura can be weakened by illness, drug and alcohol abuse, chronic depressed and negative emotions, and stress. It can also be weakened by prolonged exposure to negative energy and psychic attack. In addition, a small number of people have auras that are susceptible to outside influences. For example, empathic people, who easily absorb the emotions and thoughts of others, may have such conditions.

Auras are not invulnerable, and sometimes even strong auras can be affected by powerful and persistent psychic attack. There are many ways to keep the aura strong and healthy, and there are remedies that can be undertaken if the aura becomes vulnerable.

Characteristics of the aura

Auras radiate from everything in nature: minerals, plants, animals and humans. The aura is not visible to ordinary vision but can be seen clairvoyantly. It often appears as a multi-colored mist that fades into space with no definite boundary. It has sparks, rays and streamers.

The emanation of vital energy from life forms has been known since ancient times, appearing in the writings and art of Egypt, India, Greece and Rome. In the 16th century, Paracelsus was one of the first Western scholars to expound upon the astral body, a part of the aura, which he described as a "fiery globe."

In the 18th century, the clairvoyant Emanuel Swedenborg said in his *Spiritual Diary* that "there is a spiritual sphere surrounding everyone, as well as a natural and corporal one."

The Importance of the Aura

Scientific study of the aura began in the late 18th century, when Franz Anton Mesmer put forth the theory of "animal magnetism," an electromagnetic force that could be transmitted from one person to another and be healing. (This is what Dr. Berridge did with his magnetic hand passes – a transference of vital energy.)

In 1845, Baron Karl von Reichenbach, a German chemist, announced the discovery of the Odic force energy. Reichenbach's clairvoyant test subjects sat in darkened rooms and saw flame-like energy radiating from fingertips, animals, plants, magnets and crystals. The subjects described seeing flames of red, orange, green and violet, which alternately appeared and disappeared; a violet red, which disappeared in a smoke-like vapor; and intermingled sparks and stars among all colors.

Shortly before World War I, Dr. Walter J. Kilner, who was in charge of electrotherapy at St. Thomas's Hospital in London, discovered that the human aura could be made visible if viewed through an apparatus containing a coal-tar dye called dicyanin, which made ultraviolet light visible.

Kilner saw the aura as a faint haze that sometimes separated into two or three portions, and so he believed the aura had three parts: 1) the etheric double, a transparent dark space, narrow and often obliterated by the second band; 2) the inner aura, fairly constant in size and the densest portion; and 3) the outer aura, inconstant in size, which often appeared blended into inner aura. In addition, he observed rays emanating from the bodies of healthy persons.

Kilner noticed that the aura reflected a person's state of health, and by 1919 he formulated a method of auric diagnosis of illness. In some cases, the aura is affected only locally, where disease is located, while in other illnesses, the entire aura is affected. It appears out of shape, granulated, striated, dense or cloudy in the affected areas. As the patient recovers, so does the aura.

Kilner also noticed that weak, depleted auras suck off the energy of healthy, vigorous auras around them.

In psychic attack or psychic vampirism, energy can be sucked off healthy auras as well.

Clairvoyants see the aura as emanating from and interpenetrating the human body. Health and emotion show in various colors, energy patterns or breaks, and clear and cloudy spots. Colors can fluctuate, depending not only on health but also on changes in mental and emotional activity. Spiritual practice refines and strengthens the aura.

The aura bodies

The aura extends into the ether and has numerous layers, more than what Kilner perceived. There are seven primary bodies that are of importance in psychic protection.

1. The etheric body

This is the layer closest to the physical body. It both mirrors physical health and contains forewarnings of physical health issues. Illness and disease manifest first in the etheric body, sometimes months or years before physical symptoms manifest.

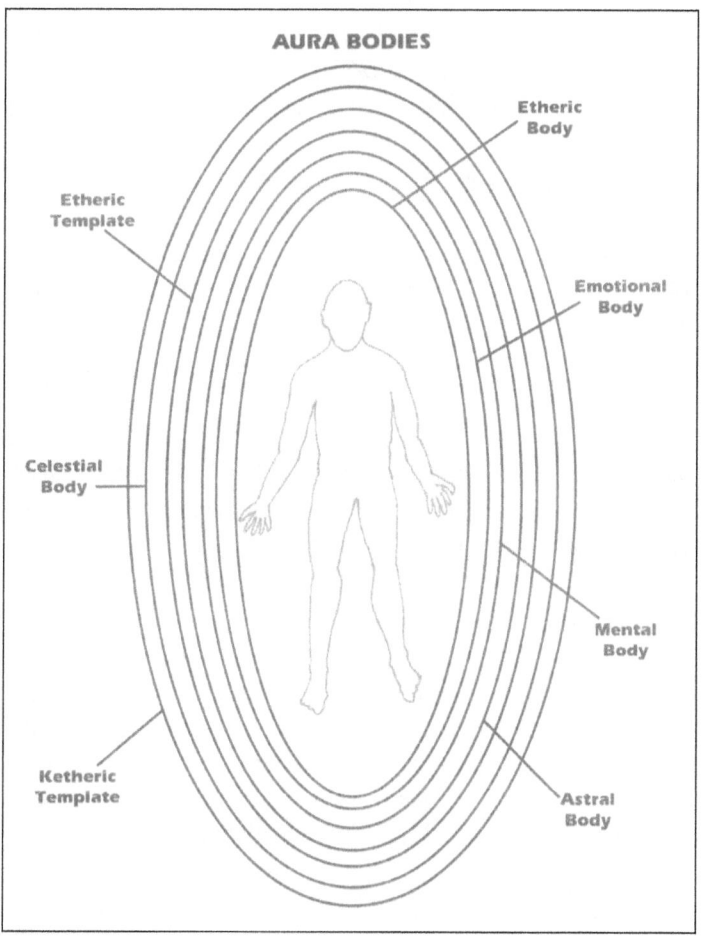

The seven primary bodies of the aura. Credit: John Weaver.

2. The emotional body

This layer contains our emotions and emotional health. All our emotions register and lodge here. Prolonged negative emotions affect the vitality of this layer, which in turn can impact other aura layers.

3. The mental body

Our thoughts and intentions are carried here, as well as our ability to take creative energy from the cosmos and turn it into manifestation.

4. The astral body

The astral cords connecting us to others are in this layer. Strong relationships strengthen this body. Broken, conflicted relationships contribute to vulnerability.

5. The etheric template

Also called the etheric double, this layer contains the blueprint of the body and who we are – our personality and self-expression. Recall that this was the aura body that Dion Fortune felt was damaged by her boss, because her self-expression and personal truth were stifled.

6. The celestial body

The celestial body is our interface with the spirit world and the divine and is nourished by unconditional love.

7. Ketheric template

This body holds the information about our past lives and soul purpose.

How psychic attack affects the aura

When psychic attack occurs, it works its way through the layers of the aura at the points of greatest vulnerability. The perpetrator attempts to make a link to the aura, usually in one or more of the four layers closest to the physical body, which then becomes a conduit for transmitting negative energy and for sucking off and depleting the vital force of the victim.

Links can be established in a variety of ways. Sometimes it is through the eyes, as described in the chapter on Malevolent Stares. Sometimes it is through the victim's own vulnerabilities created by poor physical, emotional and mental health or alcohol/drug abuse. (Note: poor health alone is not an open door to psychic attack but may in certain cases be an important factor.) Links can be formed through engagements in spirit activity, such as sorcery or summoning low-level spirits. Links also can be formed through sexual activity.

Some paranormal investigators may acquire negative spirit attachments to their auras from cases and places they investigate. Investigation alone will not result in attachment; most investigators never have an issue. However, some who engage in questionable practices, such as extreme provocation ("Come on, hit me, show me what you've got!"), issue an open invitation to trouble. Other investigators may not realize they are at risk for reasons unique to their circumstances.

The first part of the aura to be impacted is spiritual health. The victim may start to feel disconnected spiritually, or doubt religious views, or become vulnerable to or attracted to low-spirit activity. He or she may feel alienated from others.

Attachments are then made in the astral body.

The next level is penetration of the mental body. The victim may feel foreign or intrusive thoughts, or "thoughts that are not my own." There may even be impressions of an outside voice impressing itself on one's own voice or inner thoughts. These intrusions may reinforce the "worthlessness" of the victim or urge the victim to take harmful or violent actions toward self or others.

When the emotional body is hit, feelings of worthlessness and hopelessness escalate. The victim may fall into deep depression.

Emotional and mental influences are often called "oppression," one of the stages of possession.

When the etheric body is affected, the victim is in danger of full physical possession. Physical health deteriorates, and victims may be influenced to eat and do things that endanger them bodily.

Depending on the circumstances, progression through the aura may occur over time or may happen all at once.

If a negative impact is the result of an established or long-term relationship that has become toxic, there will

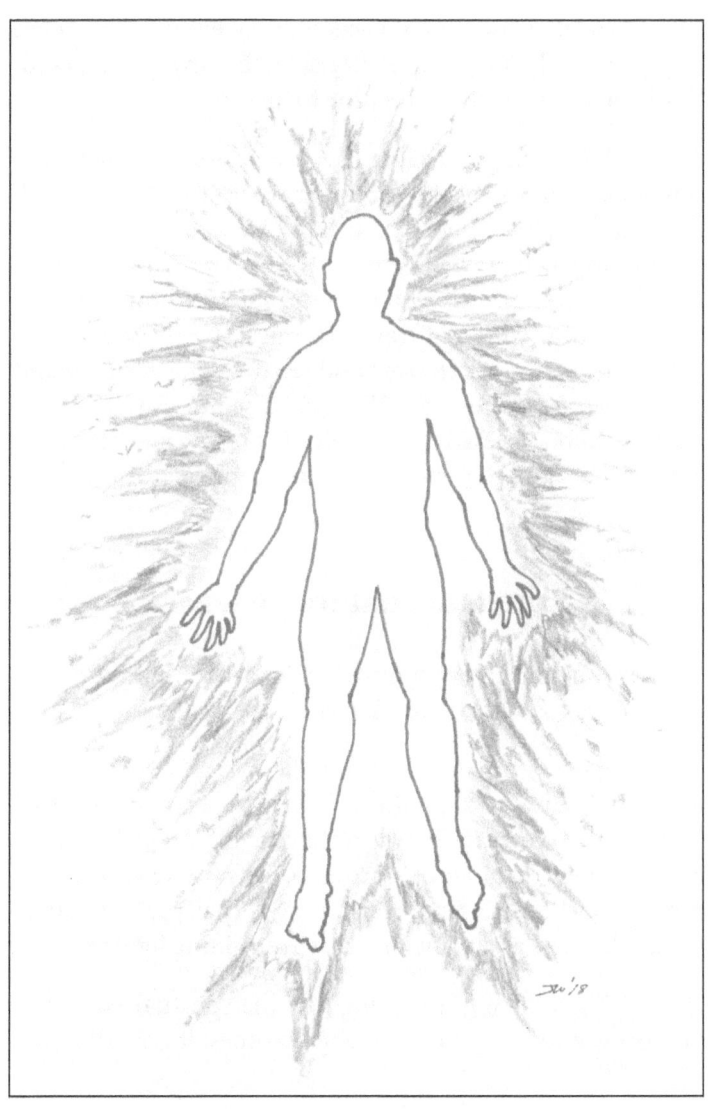

A weakened aura has rough, jagged edges and thin spots. Credit: John Weaver.

be connecting energy cords that will need to be addressed. All our relationships establish cords of energy. The more important and longer the relationship, the stronger the cord. Cords can even last from lifetime to lifetime.

Some energy healers, spirit releasers and exorcists can detect aura issues by scanning where the aura is weak and vulnerable, where intrusions have been made by psychic attack, and where energy cords to toxic people exist. Attachments show up as holes in the aura or things sticking into the aura, such as straw-like tubes, barbs and hooks. Attachments can be removed and repaired energetically and may need to be combined with other remedies as well. Energy cords can be severed or dissolved. Sometimes attaching entities hide, and so the aura must be scanned again.

Protecting natural defenses

The best way to keep your aura barrier at optimum function is to stay in good health on all levels of being.

It is especially important to pay attention to the spiritual body, the first line of defense. Have a spiritual foundation to your life. It may be the religion of your family, or it may be new religious or spiritual beliefs you have acquired throughout life. The important thing is that you have some spiritual beliefs and principles that are guiding lights.

The best way to strengthen the spiritual body and the entire aura cuts across all religious lines. It is meditation.

Meditation is different from prayer, in which a request is made, or a dialogue is conducted with a higher spiritual force. Meditation is a stilling of the mind, which makes a different kind of transcendent spiritual connection.

Meditation practices have developed in both East and West over many centuries, both within and outside of religious practices. There are different forms of meditation, and no "right" or "wrong" way.

You may think that meditation requires extended periods of time. Monks, ascetics and adepts throughout the ages have engaged in long meditations, but the average person, in today's busy world, can easily adapt techniques to suit time demands. Even a short time – 10 to 15 minutes – will yield great results when done daily.

I find that the best time to meditate is before I start my day and the brain gets too busy. I sit down, put on some soft meditational music, and still my mind and body. As thoughts arise, I release them like water flowing through a sieve. I usually hold an intention, such as being completely at peace and in harmony and balance with Everything That Is. As my breath comes into the body, I visualize it filling me with golden white light from the Godhead or Source of All Being.

Technically, this is a form of "active meditation." In Eastern traditions, the complete emptying of the mind is sought. I believe active meditation is better suited to the modern Western mind, because it does involve a clearing and stilling, but provides a beneficial mental focus as well.

Years ago, I learned Zen meditation, and enjoyed it so much that over time I incorporated it into other elements of meditation that I practice. The release of thoughts like water flowing through a sieve is a Zen approach to meditation. Zen recognizes that thoughts will arise, and they can be released. Another way to release thoughts is to focus the mind on the image of a pearl.

Sometimes I use my meditation periods to focus on goals by visualizing them as already accomplished.

Regardless of how you meditate, the bottom line is that meditation brings a powerful infusion of high-level spiritual energy into all levels of your being. It is like going to the psychic gym and having your aura pump weights.

Elsewhere in this book I discuss other ways to boost psychic protection, such as with amulets. While they are effective, they will not do the protection job alone if you have neglected your energetic and spiritual health. Reciting a prayer to which you feel no energetic link will not be of much help to you, for example.

The objections I hear the most from people when I mention meditation are, "I don't have the time!" and "It's impossible for me to quiet my mind." These are false objections.

When something is supremely important to you, do you make the time to do it? Of course. If maintaining your spiritual health is important to you, you will make certain you have the time to look after it. Get up a few minutes earlier in the morning. Make some time before you retire at the end of the day. Be flexible. Schedules vary. If you miss in the morning, find a few minutes of quiet time at lunch or at the end of the day.

The second objection, that it is impossible to quiet the mind, likewise has no basis. Everyone can, with a bit of effort, learn how to clear mental clutter. No one expects you to meditate like a yogi straight out of the starting gate. Sadly, our modern culture conditions us to be constantly distracted by noise and racket. A lot of people do not know what it is like to be in a quiet environment.

Quieting the mind is especially important for another reason: manifestation. The ability to bring things into manifestation starts at the spiritual level with creativity and vision, and then goes to the mental level where thought and intention condition action. If you are constantly at the mercy of mental chaos fostered by our noise-happy culture, how can you focus any internal power to accomplish your goals, let alone stay balanced and happy?

The chakras

In addition to benefitting the aura, meditation has a positive effect on the chakras.

Chakras are wheel-shaped interfaces that funnel the universal life force into the body and the aura envelope around it. "Chakra" is a Sanskrit term for "wheel." They are shaped like multi-colored lotus petals or spoked wheels that whirl at various speeds as they process the universal life force.

Chakras play a vital role, distributing the universal life force throughout the physical, emotional, mental and spiritual bodies, thus promoting good aura strength and health. They are invisible to ordinary sight but may be perceived clairvoyantly. Through meditation and energy healing, they can be balanced, cleansed and stimulated.

Psychic attack can adversely affect the chakras as well as the rest of the aura.

There are hundreds of chakras throughout the body, but we are usually concerned with seven primary ones that are aligned approximately along the spinal column, from the root, or base of the spine, to the crown, or top of the head. Each chakra governs a different aspect of life, as well as different physical and psycho-spiritual functions. The chakras are increasingly complex the further up the spinal column they are. Each has a different color. When chakras are well-balanced, they rotate smoothly, and their colors are clear and not cloudy.

I learned how to perceive the chakras by developing my intuition and studying energy healing. Energy healers can see how chakras are clogged; sometimes the culprits are old emotional baggage. Old wounds and unresolved issues remain in our energy fields, sometimes for many years.

Chakras also can reveal how thoughts and belief patterns are manifesting. As I mentioned, thought creates reality; we become what we think, and we attract to us what we think. If you want to change your outer house, you have to first set your inner house in order.

In meditation, you can focus on the chakras, bringing spiritual energy into them.

Here is a summary of the seven primary chakras:

First Chakra (Root)
Color: Red

The root chakra encompasses the basic levels of life: self-preservation, one's animal nature, taste and smell, and needs for food, shelter, safety and security. It governs the physical body and gaining a foothold in the material world. It also relates to environment – family and cultural, ethnic and racial expectations. Here we find our core beliefs and code of honor: our view of how the world ought to treat us, what we deserve and how we should get what we deserve. Such conditioning is crucial, for it affects our outlook throughout life, and how successful we are likely to be in achieving our goals and desires.

Second Chakra (Sacral or Spleen)
Color: Orange

The second or spleen chakra holds sexual energy, instincts, passions, ambitions and the desire to attract and possess both people and things. The spleen chakra is linked to the lower astral plane of instincts. Spleen chakra energy is assertive and risk-taking. It is also controlling. Money, power, possessions and people can all become pawns to serve passions and desires. We define ourselves by what we have.

Third Chakra (Solar Plexus)
Color: Yellow

Emotions, feelings of attraction and desire for union are uppermost in the third chakra. It is the point where astral energy enters the aura's etheric field. The solar plexus chakra affects the adrenal glands, pancreas, liver and stomach. It corresponds to the upper astral plane, which contains our self-esteem, inner power, sense of responsibility and honesty.

When the third chakra is balanced, we know our emotions with great honesty, and we have self-esteem: we are

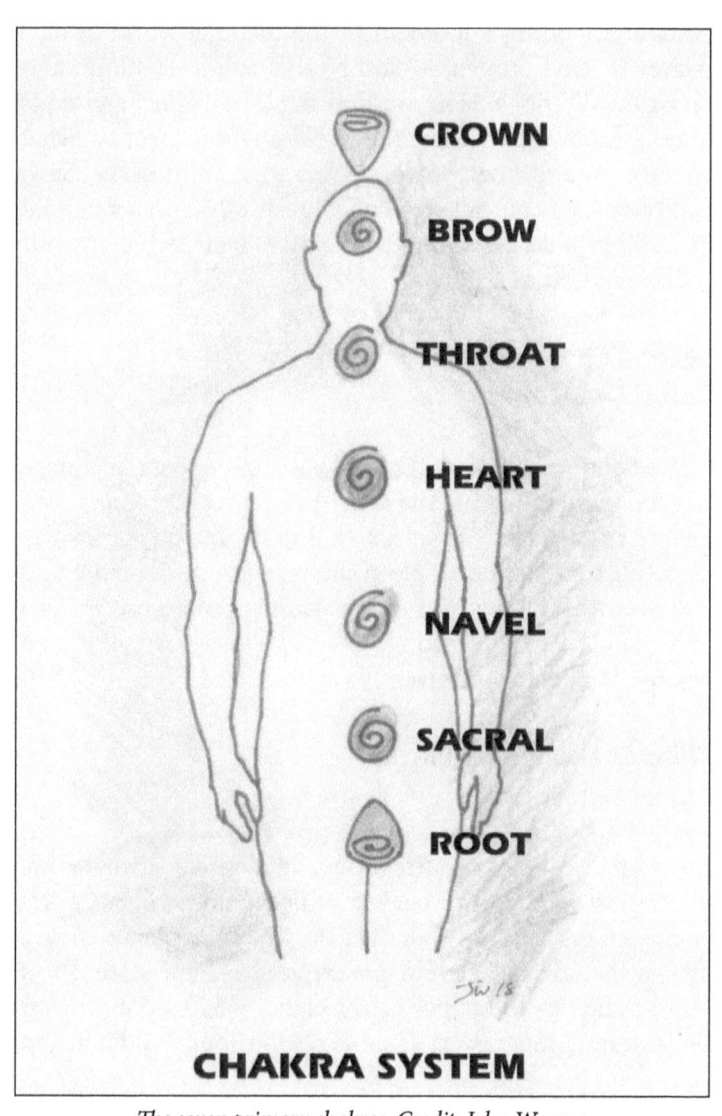

The seven primary chakras. Credit: John Weaver.

comfortable with ourselves, and confident in our gifts that we have to offer to another. We resolve and heal emotional wounds. We do not carry wounds and grudges with us.

Fourth Chakra (Heart)
Color: Green

The heart chakra governs the thymus gland and influences immunity to disease. It is the first chakra linked to higher consciousness, and concerns love, understanding, forgiveness, compassion and selflessness. It encompasses the lower level of the mental plane, which concerns memory and concrete thinking. The fourth chakra lies between the lower three chakras and the upper three chakras, and thus is the turning point in spirituality. When the heart center fully awakens to love, we have an awareness of a bigger picture, an awareness that is more subtle and refined.

Fifth Chakra (Throat)
Color: Blue

The fifth or throat chakra takes us into the upper mental plane, into abstract thought and contemplation. It is associated with creativity and self-expression and the search for truth. It also influences the thyroid and parathyroid glands and metabolism and is associated with certain states of expanded consciousness. The throat center expresses one's true voice.

Sixth Chakra (Brow)
Color: Indigo

The sixth or brow chakra – also called the third eye – governs the opening of the psychic senses and spiritual vision. Here is the center of faith: we see the unseen, the potential, and know that we can bring it into manifestation. We see into the realms of spirit; we understand mystical subtleties that go beyond the description of words.

The sixth chakra is concerned with learning the big picture – the relationship of the soul to God, and to the All That Is, our immortality, past lives, and destinies.

Seventh Chakra (Crown)
Color: Purple

The seventh or crown chakra reaches into the upper spiritual plane, where pure spirit, absolute harmony and oneness exist. In mystical traditions, the opening of the crown chakra brings enlightenment and the experience of the boundless oneness. All things flow back to the One. There is no more "I" or "we." The seventh chakra corresponds to the seventh spiritual plane of oneness, which Dion Fortune described as the "All are One and One is All."

In sacred art, the activated crown chakra is represented by the halo and crowns or domes of light.

Chapter 4

Aura Defenses

Aura visualizations and martial arts

On a daily basis, and as part of your meditation, protect the aura by visualizing yourself in an egg-shaped shell of divine white light. The shell allows everything beneficial to pass through but deflects negative energy, attacks and thoughts. If stronger protection is required, visualize yourself encased in armor. Some people prefer to visualize a shell of mirrors to reflect the negative energy back.

Laine Robinson, a quantum healing therapist, shared one of her clearing techniques with me:

> *Bring in the white light from above, (God, Higher Power). Then bring in red light Earth energy from below. Spiral them within your body. When you are totally full, keep filling in your aura until you feel lighter. It will help to keep you protected and will shake off some unwanted entities such as elementals. You can also use it to fill and clear areas in a house.*

For added protection put a layer of violet light underneath the white light, next to the body. The violet light is a vibration of spiritual strength. It is associated with the violet flame of the Ascended Master St. Germain and is a shield of truth, freedom, justice, mercy and transmutation. The violet light can be projected out through the hands as well, as an extra defensive measure.

Mack Harris, a "spiritual warrior" who battles dark forces on the astral plane, makes use of violet light. He offers this advice:

> *When you meditate, place your hands upright with palms together. Create within them a ball of violet chi energy. Make that ball expand up your arm, then around your body. If you can cover your body, you will have a shield that nothing so far has been able to penetrate. If you can make the shield, then see if you can project it outwards. Remember, the energy is from the universe, rather than from you.*

I use violet light as an extra layer and projected force and find it quite effective.

Dr. Edward C. Berringer used a visualization of life force energy to end a case of psychic vampirism. A woman who consulted him said she felt ill and exhausted whenever she was in the presence of a certain man who suffered from bad health. Berringer believed the man was deliberately vampirizing the woman to try to improve his own health. He obtained a description of the man and then did a ritual using visualization. He saw the man and woman facing each other, and he placed a shield of universal life force around the woman. The psychic vampirism stopped.

The aura can be pushed out as a defensive measure by using breath and visualization. Draw in the universal life force in white or white and violet light through the intake of breath, and on the outflow of breath visualize the aura widening out around you. This can be done quickly on a short expelling of breath. You can also add spikes to the aura, and mental commands such as "Keep away!"

You can blast violet energy from your hands as a protective measure, too, and expand violet depth around your aura field.

I also take measures with the chakras and mental activity, especially after doing a paranormal investigation. I visualize shutters over the chakras and mentally pull a string down to close the shutters, allowing unwanted or excess energy to flow into the earth. Similarly, I pull the shutters down around mental activity to prevent spirits or entities from linking to and being energized by thought. I then engage in a light, distracting activity, such as comedy on television.

Laughter and humor are excellent ways to deflect and break up negativity.

If you are experiencing sleep disturbances, reinforce aura shielding with white and violet light prior to retiring.

Body actions and postures

The aura can be shielded by body actions and postures. If you feel you are or have been in the presence of negative energy, ground yourself. This can be accomplished by placing the palms on wood, or shaking energy off the hands, or using the breath. (If wood is not available, any solid surface will suffice.) Breathe in golden white light and send it down through the body and out the soles of the feet into the earth.

You can protect your aura by closing off energy circuits. When sitting, cross your feet at the ankles and fold your hands or lace your fingers over your solar plexus. When standing, cross your arms over your midriff and pull your chakra shutters down. Reinforce the shell of divine white/violet light around you.

Bodywork and measures

Salt baths and showers with salt scrubs will take care of a lot of clingy negative energy in the aura. Dion Fortune recommended a hot water bottle on the solar plexus to help restore vitality.

Mustard hot water footbaths are reputed to draw toxins out of the body and restore vitality. Here are the ingredients to make four baths:

- 1 cup baking soda
- ¼ cup mustard powder
- 6 drops wintergreen or peppermint essential oil
- 6 drops rosemary essential oil
- 6 drops eucalyptus essential oil

Place all ingredients in a storage jar (such as used for canning) and whisk together. Add four tablespoons to a running bath and swish around to disperse the powder. For a foot soak, use one to two tablespoons.

Another footbath formula that cleanses and restores uses sea salt instead of mustard powder:

- ½ cup baking soda
- ½ cup sea salt
- few drops essential oil(s) of choice

I especially like lavender essential oil for its calming properties. Other favorite relaxing oils are mandarin, bergamot, ylang ylang, and chamomile.

For energy and revitalization, I like rosemary, eucalyptus, lemon, geranium (a good balancer), tea tree and peppermint.

There are many other oils including blends, and an aromatherapy expert or guidebook can help you choose. Apply the oils to the water, never directly on the skin. Essential oils are strong and can burn skin; they must be diluted in water or a carrier oil.

In addition, massage, acupuncture, medical chi gong and other forms of bodywork also are beneficial. For removal of aura attachments and energy cords, consult a professional, such as an energy healer.

Mental and emotional monitoring

Pay more attention to your thoughts and feelings, which have a powerful effect upon the aura. If you are not full of negativity, you will have no "food" for negative people and entities. Immediately replace anything negative with something positive. Visualize a happy scene or relive happy emotions.

You can also repeat affirmations:

- I open my inner guidance and deepest wisdom.
- I align my consciousness with the Source.
- I live in the light of truth.
- I am a channel for truth and unconditional love.
- I have complete clarity of mind and unlimited vision.
- I am in harmony and balance with all of creation.

Incorporate affirmations into your daily meditation practice.

Countering negative thoughtforms

Thoughtforms created and directed by ritual require the help of someone knowledgeable in those arts. Thoughtforms generated by ill will and hostility can be deflected, countered and dissipated with defensive, positive thoughtforms, aura martial arts and body postures.

Thoughtforms created by the victim through repressed anger, depression and other emotions, which then turn on the victim, may first require traditional counseling.

The best thoughtform is a healthy, happy state of mind, and ample doses of humor.

Theosophists Annie Besant and Charles W. Leadbeater stressed that regular meditation is important in cultivating positive thoughtforms. The meditation sends out a stream of magnetism that continues to work long after the meditation is ended.

We can also take a cue from the New Thought movement, which arose in the 19th century and emphasized the creative and spiritual power of thought. Science of Mind, founded by Ernest Holmes, teaches that we are surrounded by an Infinite Intelligence, or Mind (God), which functions upon our beliefs. If we let go of destructive thoughts and replace them with constructive ones, we enter a cooperation with this Mind that enables us to be healthier, happier, more successful and more spiritually fulfilled.

To this end, daily affirmations, meditation and prayer facilitate that objective. In magical terms, these activities create positive thoughtforms that manifest in the physical world.

Holmes taught that there is but one Mind and everything is an aspect of it; each of us uses a portion of It. He taught, "My thought is in control of my experience and I can direct my thinking" and "the ability to control my experiences and have them result in happiness, prosperity and success lies in my own mind and my use of it."

"Mind responds to mind," said Holmes. "It is done to you as you believe." In other words, do not *ask* for things, but *declare* them. This is the Law of Mind, which manifests the beliefs we speak into It.

To improve health and for healing, Holmes recommended meditation upon affirmations such as "God-life surges through my entire body," or "I am well and successful in everything that I do," followed by a period of prayer in which the supplicant does not ask for anything, but declares desired results, accepts them as though they have manifested and gives thanks for them.

This method can be applied to any situation or need in life. One's thoughts and motives ideally should be God-like. A key element is belief in the desired results. Holmes stressed that belief must be felt with the total being. He noted that the effective prayer is one prayed by a person whose faith has removed all doubt.

Righteous anger and will

There are times when anger is the most effective mental defense. Every person is a sovereign being, and no other person – or entity – has the right to breach one's natural boundaries to interfere in free will and self-determination. The use of aura defenses described above establish and reinforce that sovereignty. Combine those with will power and righteous anger to repel the unwanted. Examples are "Get away! You have no right to bother me! Leave!" You must be forceful and have a clear visualization of your boundaries. There are absolutely no entry points in any sphere of your life for anything unwanted.

Should psychic attack be returned?

Opinions differ on the handling of psychic attack energy. These are possible actions to take:

- Neutralize the energy and let it go.
- Send the energy into the earth or the angelic realm for healing.
- Return the energy to the sender.
- Take no action.

Many people feel justified in returning the energy to the sender. Others feel they are doing a positive service by directing it to a healing force.

Dion Fortune advised taking no action. When good protection barriers are in place, the energy will not reach its target. It will then, by cosmic law, return to its sender. In *Psychic Self-Defense*, she stated:

> *It is a well-known cosmic law that everything moves in circles, and whatever forces we send out, and whatever thoughtforms we extrude*

from our auras, unless absorbed by the object to which they are directed, will return to us in due course. One of the most effective, and also one of the most widely practiced methods of occult defense is to refuse to react to an attack, neither accepting nor neutralizing the forces projected against one, and thus turning them back on their sender. We must never overlook the fact that a so-called occult attack may be evil thoughtforms returning home to roost.

I agree in part with Fortune. We must defend ourselves as we see fit, and then turn it over to the divine.

Chapter 5

Calling On Spiritual Forces

Your regular habits of protection should include help from spiritual allies.

Angels

Angels, God's emissaries in the world and all creation, are considered some of our best spiritual allies. They are messengers linking humanity and the Godhead. They carry prayers to God and the answers back. They are enforcers of God's will. In Biblical times, angels were known to punish as well as assist. In addition, angels help to hold the cosmic order in place.

Angels are powerful spiritual forces for protection and banishment.

The Bible makes no specific reference to the creation of angels, but many theologians say their creation is implied in Genesis 1:1: "In the beginning God created the heavens and the earth." Throughout the Old Testament, there are numerous references to angels interacting with people upon instructions from God. In the New Testament, angels have more of a supporting role as Jesus Christ takes center stage and becomes the primary intermediary.

Angels are specific to Christianity, Judaism and Islam, but their roots go much deeper. The *malakh* (messenger) of the early Hebrews was an amalgam of intermediary, tutelary and protective spirits the Hebrews encountered in their exposure to the mix of Middle Eastern and Mediterranean cultures, among them Babylonia, Persia, Egypt, Sumeria and Greece. The term "angel" derives from the Greek term *angelos*, or "messenger." Christianity absorbed the Judaic angel, and Islam in turn absorbed the Christian angel.

As Christianity developed, concepts of angels were codified, and theologians debated their appearances, ability to be physical, and even whether they ate human food. They were organized into hierarchies. Their numbers were debated. Conclusion: There are as many angels as are necessary.

Most angels are unnamed. The Bible references only Michael and Gabriel by name, and the Catholic canon adds a third, Raphael. A wealth of names, functions and duties of angels comes from writers outside the canon of the Church, such as the authors of the Book of Enoch and Jubilees.

The wings of angels demonstrate their otherworldly nature and distinct difference from human beings. However, wings are more of an artistic interpretation than reality. In the Bible, angels are described as shining men or beings. The Hebrews have no images of angels. The Greeks gave their messenger gods small wings, usually on their heads, helmets or feet, to represent their ability to access celestial realms. As angel art developed in Christianity, wings evolved from scrawny little things on backs to giant, swan-like wings.

In modern times, most people experience angels as pillars of light or "mysterious strangers" disguised as human beings. Some people report wings in the shape of the light they see, and a minority report wings – perhaps because angels are portrayed that way in art and thus are expected to have wings.

The hierarchy of angels

People like to organize themselves, and societies and governments are structured with different levels of authority and power. Early humankind figured that the celestial realms had to be organized as well: the heavens and earth reflected each other.

Numerous hierarchies of angels were conceived, but the one that stuck and was accepted into Christianity was a nine-tier structure credited to a man of the 5th or early 6th century called Pseudo-Dionysius. The "Pseudo" didn't mean he was false; rather, it distinguished him from a Biblical personality known as Dionysius. Pseudo-Dionysius was a Christian and a Platonic philosopher.

Pseudo-Dionysius's hierarchy of nine levels is divided into three triads that are sometimes called "choirs."

The top tier are the angels closest to God, so refined that humans rarely perceive them, and the bottom tier are the angels closest to earth, the ones we perceive and call upon. We can petition angels at any of the levels, however, so it is useful to know who they are and their functions and duties.

Tier I

Angels – The lowest order of angels seems mighty to us. These are the workhorses for humanity that include our personal guardian angels who are involved in our prayers and daily lives, and the so-called "mysterious strangers" who appear at times of crisis.

Archangels – The second level features the familiar figures of named angels, such as Michael, Gabriel, Raphael and Uriel. Archangels can stand in the presence of God – an overpowering energy to most beings – and they are concerned with a higher order. They represent ideal qualities and characteristics such as strength, valor, healing and visionary capacity. Michael is the most frequently invoked in spiritual safety, and more about him will follow.

Principalities – These angels are concerned with large groups of people, such as communities, races and nations. Peace and harmony are their bywords.

Tier II

Powers – The powers embody and represent the right use of power and authority. They can be called upon when we need an extra ounce of persistence, the ability to manage things well, and the skill to persuade others.

Virtues – Think Biblical graces and the beatitudes. Virtues concern mercy, forgiveness, gratitude and miracles.

Dominations (also Dominions) – The dominations combine the qualities of the powers and virtues: the exercising of power with grace.

Tier III

Thrones – These angels are literally the chariots – or, in modern terms, vehicles – for Godly energy, which they carry throughout creation. They are concerned with divine justice and are fonts of creativity and inspiration.

Cherubim – The cherubim represent knowledge, spiritual wisdom, truth, enlightenment, discernment and revelation. They embody the capacity to envision.

Seraphim – The highest order of angels holds the unconditional love and intense light of the Godhead and helps to disperse them throughout creation by powering the intense vibrations to levels that can be perceived and absorbed by all things. They are fiery in nature and represent purification.

The archangels of protection

There are three archangels we are mostly likely to rely upon in battling dark forces: Michael, Gabriel and Raphael. They have all been named saints by the Catholic Church. In addition, there is a fourth archangel, Uriel, who completes the foundation of primary archangels.

Michael

Michael is the most prominent and greatest angel in Christian, Hebrew and Islamic lore. The name Michael means in Hebrew "who is like God" or "who is as God." Michael is Chaldean in origin.

His chief roles are warrior, priest, protector, healer and guardian. He is chief of the orders of virtues and archangels; one of the angels of the presence of God; a prince of light; angel of truth; and angel of repentance, righteousness, mercy and salvation.

Christianity recognizes Michael as the angel who wages ceaseless war against the forces of Satan. He is the special defender of Christians and the Church. Satan trembles at the mere mention of his name, and all the angels of heaven bow down before him in obedience. Michael inspires fidelity to God.

In Catholic devotion, there is no greater angel than Michael, the "Prince of the heavenly hosts." Churches were built and dedicated to him from the 5th century on. So intense was adoration of Michael that many devotional cults sprang up all over Europe, peaking in popularity in the late Middle Ages. Devotion to Michael is still practiced today.

At Mass, Michael presides over the worship of adoration to the Most High, and sends to God the prayers of the faithful, symbolized by the smoke from incense. The prayer to St. Michael asking him to defend Christians in battle is a condensed form of the general exorcism against Satan and evil spirits, composed by Pope Leo XIII (r. 1878-1903), and is given below.

In art, iconography and statuary, Michael is most often shown in battle garb, holding a shield and sword. The shield protects, and the sword is both a weapon and a symbol of discernment, the ability to know and cut right from wrong. He is also depicted trampling upon Satan and holding his sword over him and chains to bind him.

One of Michael's important duties is guiding the souls of the newly departed to the afterlife, where he weighs the souls for righteousness.

Michael shares with Raphael special healing duties, a function naturally associated with him as protector of the general welfare.

Michael can be called upon for protection and when anything negative needs to be banished from an environment or detached from the aura. He is often accompanied by his band of warrior angels. He can also be invoked for courage, strength, determination and persistence.

Many paranormal investigators invoke the Prayer to the Archangel Michael – Pope Leo XIII's condensed exorcism – prior to investigating, especially at sites known to have negative presences and activity. The prayer can be used at any time for protection:

> *Holy Michael, the Archangel, defend us in battle. Be our safeguard against the*

wickedness and snares of the devil. May God rebuke him, we humbly pray; and do you, O Prince of the heavenly host, by the power of God cast into hell Satan and all the evil spirits who wander through the world seeking the ruin of souls. Amen.

Raphael

The archangel St. Raphael has important functions in exorcism and healing. His name means "healer" or "doctor"; Raphael is "the shining one who heals" and "the medicine of God." He is often connected with a potent symbol of healing, the serpent. He is entrusted with the physical well-being of the earth and its inhabitants.

Raphael is one of the few angels who can stand in the presence of God. He belongs to four orders of angels: seraphim, cherubim, dominations and powers. He is the angel of the evening winds; guardian of the Tree of Life; and the angel of prayer, peace, joy, light and love.

Raphael's exorcism skills are related in the Book of Tobit, which is included in the Catholic Bible but not the Protestant Bible.

The Book of Tobit was originally written in Hebrew or Aramaic, probably in the 2nd century BCE. The story concerns a pious man, Tobit, and his son, Tobias. It takes place in the late 8th century BCE in the Assyrian capital of Nineveh.

By his own description, Tobit was a model of piety, walking "in the ways of truth and righteousness." When he was 50 years old, he broke rules for handling a corpse and as a consequence was rendered blind by bird droppings that fell into his eyes. After eight years of living in despair, Tobit begged God to let him die. In preparation for his end, he called in his only son and told him to journey to far-away Media, where he had left some money in trust with another man. He instructed Tobias to find a man to accompany him on the journey, and he would pay the man.

Meanwhile, in Media, a young woman named Sarah was possessed by the demon Asmodeus, "the destroyer." Sarah had attempted seven times to marry, but the demon killed each groom on the wedding night before the marriage could be consummated. Sarah's father, Raguel, prayed to God for relief.

God heard the prayers of both Tobit and Raguel, and dispatched Raphael to heal Tobit's blindness and exorcise the demons from Sarah. Raphael, disguised as a man (a "mysterious stranger"), joined Tobias on his journey to Media.

On the first evening, Raphael gave Tobias a lesson in exorcism. They camped along the Tigris River, and Tobias caught a fish for dinner.

Raphael said, "Cut open the fish and take the heart and liver and gall and put them away safely." Tobias did this. They then roasted and ate the rest of the fish.

Tobias asked the angel what use were the parts that were saved. Raphael replied, "As for the heart and the liver, if a demon or evil spirit gives trouble to anyone, you make a smoke from these before the man or woman, and that person will never be troubled again. And as for the gall, anoint with it a man who has white films in his eyes, and he will be cured."

When they arrived at Media, Raphael instructed Tobias to become betrothed to Sarah. Tobias, having learned about Sarah's possession and the unhappy fate of her previous husbands, was reluctant to do so, but he obeyed.

Raphael told him, "When you enter the bridal chamber, you shall take live ashes of incense and lay upon them some of the heart and liver of the fish so as to make a smoke. Then the demon will smell it and flee away and will never again return. And when you approach her, rise up, both of you, and cry out to the merciful God, and he will save you and have mercy on you. Do not be afraid, for she was destined for you from eternity. You will save her, and she will go with you, and I suppose you will have children by her."

The events happened as Raphael predicted. When exposed to the smoke of the burning fish heart and liver, Asmodeus fled.

Tobias and Sarah were successfully married. When they returned to Nineveh, Raphael told Tobias how to use the fish gall to anoint his father's eyes and heal his blindness.

The angel then revealed his identity. "I am Raphael, one of the seven holy angels who present the prayers of the saints and enter in the presence of the glory of the Holy One," he said.

Tobit and Tobias were alarmed to be in the presence of an archangel and fell to the ground in fear. But Raphael assured them no harm would befall them. "For I did not come as a favor on my part, but by the will of our God," he said. "Therefore, praise him forever. All these days I merely appeared to you and did not eat or drink, but you were seeing a vision. And now give thanks to God, for I am ascending to him who sent me. Write in a book everything that has happened." Raphael vanished. And that, according to lore, is how the Book of Tobit was recorded.

Raphael is usually shown in art as a mystery companion holding a fish and walking with a young man. In other images, he holds a caduceus, a staff entwined by two serpents, which in modern times is one of the primary symbols of the medical profession.

Burning fish heart and liver is a smelly business, but some perform this exorcism rite today.

More commonly, Raphael is invoked for healing and cleansing once an exorcism has been performed.

Gabriel

Gabriel is not called upon as frequently as Michael and Raphael against the dark side, but as one of the principal angels, he should not be overlooked. His name means "hero of God" or "the mighty one" in Hebrew. Gabriel is the angel of revelation, wisdom, mercy, redemption and promise. These are valuable qualities to summon in the healing process after the expelling of an unwanted presence.

Gabriel also is one of the select angels who can stand before God. He is known primarily as an announcer and herald, for in the New Testament, he announces the coming of John the Baptist and Jesus. Thus, he announces the new, the fresh start, the redeemed beginning. His energy can be invoked into a household during a cleansing process.

In art, he is usually shown holding a lily, a symbol of purity. Although Gabriel is not specifically named as the trumpeting angel of resurrection, he is credited with that role, and is shown blowing on a trumpet. Gabriel heralds success and renewal.

Uriel

Uriel is an important archangel in ex-canonical texts, notably the Book of Enoch. His name means "fire of God" or "God is my light." In the Book of Enoch, he is a punisher of sinners. He also interprets prophecies, reveals heavenly mysteries and answers weighty questions about evil and justice. He is often portrayed as holding a flame in his open hand, which represents absolute truth.

I like the energy of Uriel, because the divine fire of absolute truth is a powerful force against dark entities. It burns away anything that is impure. Uriel can be invoked in exorcism and cleansing.

Saints

Saints are men and women whose lives, acts and sanctity elevate them to an intermediary role similar to angels. They can be called upon to provide powerful spiritual help and protection.

Saints and holy people exist in all spiritual faiths and traditions. The Catholic Church has formalized sainthood, bestowing the title posthumously on individuals whose lives meet certain requirements. There are thousands of saints all over the world, and thousands more of the lesser statuses of beatified, venerable and martyred.

Saints become known for their "specialties" or patronages. For example, St. Jude is the patron saint of lost things, impossible causes and desperate situations, and is invoked when people find themselves in tough and dire situations. During depressed housing markets, people bury statues of St. Jude on their property as a good luck draw for a sale.

Not surprisingly, the fight against evil has its saint superstars. Like angels, saints are truly nondenominational, and one does not have to practice Christianity to draw upon them.

St. Benedict

At the head of the superstar list is St. Benedict (c. 487-547), known as the "Father of Western Monasticism" and the founder of the Benedictine Order. Benedict is one of the most important saints in the canon because he brought a great deal of stability and order to the monastic life. He is also famous for his triumph over the Devil, which is what makes him important in demonology and exorcism.

Saints spent their lives purifying themselves, and, according to the hagiographies (embellished biographies), were frequently subjected to attacks from the demonic as a

St. Benedict

consequence. The Devil was always seeking ways to derail them.

Benedict is said to have withstood the onslaught of Satan and his forces throughout his entire life. His first attack came when he was a teenager and had withdrawn into a cave near Subiaco, Italy, to live as a hermit for three years. Hermits were in total withdrawal from the world and were supplied with food by others.

One day Satan, in the form of a black bird, violently attacked Benedict. The youth recognized his identity and sent the bird off by making the sign of the cross. He was seized with a temptation against holy purity. To conquer it, he undressed and rolled himself several times in thorn bushes. His remedy worked, and he said throughout his life that he never again experienced such an attack on his purity. The thorn bushes became celebrated and were regarded as relics, or holy objects. A variation of this story says that Satan came in the form of a beautiful woman instead of a black bird.

Benedict withstood other attacks. Later in his life, monks asked for his monastic leadership. Finding it too strict, they attempted to poison him with a drink, but when he prayed a blessing and made the sign of the cross over the cup, it shattered.

On another occasion, a jealous monk tried to kill Benedict with a poisoned loaf of bread, but a raven appeared, snatched it up and took it away.

Benedict is known for his *Rule*, a handbook of spiritual guidance for living a Christ-centered life, and a set of administrative rules for running a monastery. *The Rule of*

St. Benedict is still used and consulted today and adapted to modern living.

Every saint in the Catholic canon has his or her own medal, which can be purchased at churches and online. They can be worn or carried as amulets that link to the energy of a particular saint, and to the intercessory power of saints in general.

St. Benedict's medal is discussed in the chapter on Amulets.

St. Patrick

St. Patrick (c. 389-461) is credited with driving the snakes (Christian symbols of Satan) out of Ireland. Patrick's name means "warlike" and "noble," excellent qualities to call upon in the fight against evil.

Patrick was born a Roman Briton, but at age 14 he was kidnapped by Irish slavers. After six years he managed to escape on a ship, and spent time having numerous adventures in other lands. Then a dream called him to return to Ireland and help spread Christianity there. He did so and spent the rest of his life working as a missionary.

According to legend, Patrick undertook a 40-day fast on top of a hill and was attacked by demons in the forms of snakes. He was so angry that he drove them all into the sea. Thus, Ireland became snake-free.

It's a nice story, but likely not true. According to natural history experts, there are no fossil records of snakes in post-glacial Ireland, so by the time of Patrick's day, there were no snakes to drive out.

Nonetheless, there is benefit from the symbolic content of the story, and because so many people have believed it for centuries, an actual thoughtform has developed. Like Benedict, Patrick rose up fiercely against the attacks from the dark side. He can be called upon for warrior energy and inspiration.

Other religious and spiritual figures

You may have your own favorite spiritual figures to call upon for help as well as those above. For example, totem animals, guardian spirits, gods and goddesses and other high-level spiritual forces are among those that provide protection. Whatever works for you and energizes you is appropriate. In order to be effective, the spiritual connection must be strong. If it is not, it will be dry and brittle.

Naturally, if you establish a regular practice of prayer and meditation and attend to your spiritual life, you will build those strong connections and they will always be there for you.

Chapter 6

Malevolent Stares

It is said that the eyes are the windows to the soul, and no one knows that better than someone bent on psychic attack. Intense staring is one of the most common and effective techniques of psychic attack and manipulation.

The perpetrator attempts to establish direct eye contact with the victim in an unwavering stare. The eye-to-eye connection enables the attacker to make an energetic link to the victim and convey something telepathically, such as negative thoughts and instructions, and negative emotions that tear down a person's will. The contact does not have to be sustained for a long period of time to be effective.

Perhaps you've felt the withering stare of a bully or someone intent on dominating and influencing you. Even when the eye-to-eye connection is broken, the effects of it can linger. If you are repeatedly exposed to malevolent staring, such as in a relationship or workplace, the effects can be cumulative. Recall Dion Fortune's gradual breakdown under the stare-driven psychic attacks of her boss.

In *The Psychology of Witchcraft: An Account of Witchcraft, Black Magic, and the Occult* (1974), Tom Ravensdale and James Morgan describe a case of psychic attack and vampirism via malevolent staring. It concerned a young woman and her husband who were offered accommodation by an older woman whom they knew slightly. Soon after moving in, the young woman became uncomfortable by constant attention from the old landlady. She would be waiting for her to come home from work every evening, and she would find a reason to visit the young woman when the husband was not present. She would fix her with an intense gaze. She emanated an unpleasant aura.

The young woman's energy declined, and her health deteriorated. As she suffered, the old woman blossomed with vigor and vitality. The husband suggested a change of residence, but his ailing wife declined and opted instead to stay longer at work. As soon as she decreased the time spent in the old woman's house, her condition improved – and the old woman's deteriorated. Within a week or two, the old woman was bedridden.

Unfortunately, the young woman took pity on her and started caring for her. The old woman's health improved immediately, but the young woman's health declined to the point where her husband sent her to a doctor. The doctor diagnosed her as anemic and overworked and ordered her to rest and eat a better diet. She followed his instructions but made no improvement. Instead, she steadily grew worse and suffered from complete exhaustion and severe headaches.

Then the husband noticed two small red patches on her throat. The marks didn't hurt and were of unknown cause, so they were ignored.

The old woman, meanwhile, had become so rejuvenated and youthful-looking that she decided to take a trip into the country to visit relatives. During her absence, the young woman's health returned. She decided to consult a psychic.

The psychic clairvoyantly saw the old woman as a psychic vampire surrounded by an aura of evil and advised her client and her husband to depart the house immediately. They lacked the funds to do so.

When the old woman returned, the victim's health once again declined. She was so weakened that she was hospitalized. Her red marks returned and now they bled. A Spiritualist friend visited and recommended that she wear a crucifix and a ring blessed by a priest, and have her room sealed with holy water. The terrified young woman agreed. When these measures had been taken, she experienced an immediate and marked improvement in her condition.

The old woman in turn became furious and displayed an uncontrolled hatred toward her victim. But as the young woman became stronger, the old woman weakened. At last the couple were able to move out. The wife made a complete recovery.

The evil eye

One form of malevolent staring known since ancient times is the evil eye. The evil eye is a hostile or envious look – sometimes called "overlooking" – that can bring on illness, misfortune, calamity, poverty, loss of love and even death. According to lore, strangers as well as magically skilled individuals can possess the evil eye.

Evil eye beliefs exist around the world. The oldest recorded reference to the evil eye appears in the cuneiform texts of the Sumerians, Babylonians and Assyrians around 3000 BCE. The ancient Egyptians believed in it and used eye shadow and lipstick to prevent the evil eye from entering their eyes or mouths. The Bible makes references to it in both Old and New Testaments. It is among ancient Hindu folk beliefs. Evil eye superstitions have remained strong into modern times, especially in Mediterranean countries such as Italy, and in Mexico and Central America.

There are two kinds of evil eye: involuntary and deliberate. Most cases of evil eye occur involuntarily; the person casting it doesn't mean to do it and probably isn't aware of it. No revenge is sought for this hazard.

Malevolent evil eye is a form of sorcery that can bring about misfortune or catastrophe. In the Middle Ages, witches were said to give the evil eye to anyone who crossed them, and to use it to bewitch judges from convicting them.

The evil eye typically occurs when someone, especially a stranger, admires one's children, livestock or possessions, or casts anyone a lingering look. Unless immediate precautions are taken, the children get sick, the animals die, the possessions are stolen, or good fortune in business turns sour. If the evil eye cannot be warded off, the victim must turn to an adept – usually an older woman in the family – who knows a secret cure.

Besides envious glances, the evil eye comes from anyone who has unusual or different-colored eyes, such as a blue-eyed stranger in a land of brown-eyed people.

Some unfortunate souls are born with permanent evil eye, laying waste to everything they see. High-ranking people such as noblemen or clergy were often believed to be afflicted like this. Pope Pius IX (r. 1846-1878) was branded an evil eye shortly after his investiture as Pope in 1846. Driving through Rome in an open car, he glanced at a nurse holding a child in an open window. Minutes later, the child fell to its death. From then on, it seemed that everything the Pope blessed resulted in disaster. Pope Leo XIII (r. 1878-1903) was also said to possess the evil eye because of the number of cardinals who died while he was in office.

In folklore, the evil eye is most likely to strike when one is happiest; good fortune, it seems, invites bad fortune. The same factors apply today. For example, neighbors, relatives and coworkers become jealous of someone's success and possessions and give the evil eye.

Malevolent gazes from entities

Shadow people, demonic beings and other hostile entities and spirits can manifest in forms with eyes, usually red. Figures that show up at bedside, or leap upon people in bed in attack, may especially have eyes that seem to bore into victims. It may be hard for victims to look away, as sometimes the power of the gaze is mesmerizing, and it establishes an energetic link. Sometimes the entity has no visible eyes, yet the victim feels the energy of the malevolent stare.

The victim should, at the earliest opportunity, visualize the staring link dissolving or shattering. In cases of repeated attacks, it may be necessary to visit an energy healer for aura repair. Repeated attacks also require help to determine the cause of the problem, and additional remedies.

Remedies

The traditional remedy to thwart the evil eye is an amulet worn or carried on the body; they vary by culture and region. The ancient Egyptians used an eye to fight an eye. The Udjat Eye, also called the Eye of God and Eye of Horus, appears on amulets, pottery and in art, warding off the forces of darkness.

The Romans used phallic symbols to ward off the evil eye, and one modern version of that is a horn-shaped amulet. A popular amulet is the "fig," a clenched fist with thumb thrust between the index and middle fingers, which also suggests a phallus.

Similarly, garlic and shamrocks are folk remedies that divert the baleful influence of the evil eye. Spitting either onto the ground or into the folds of a garment also is an old neutralizing remedy.

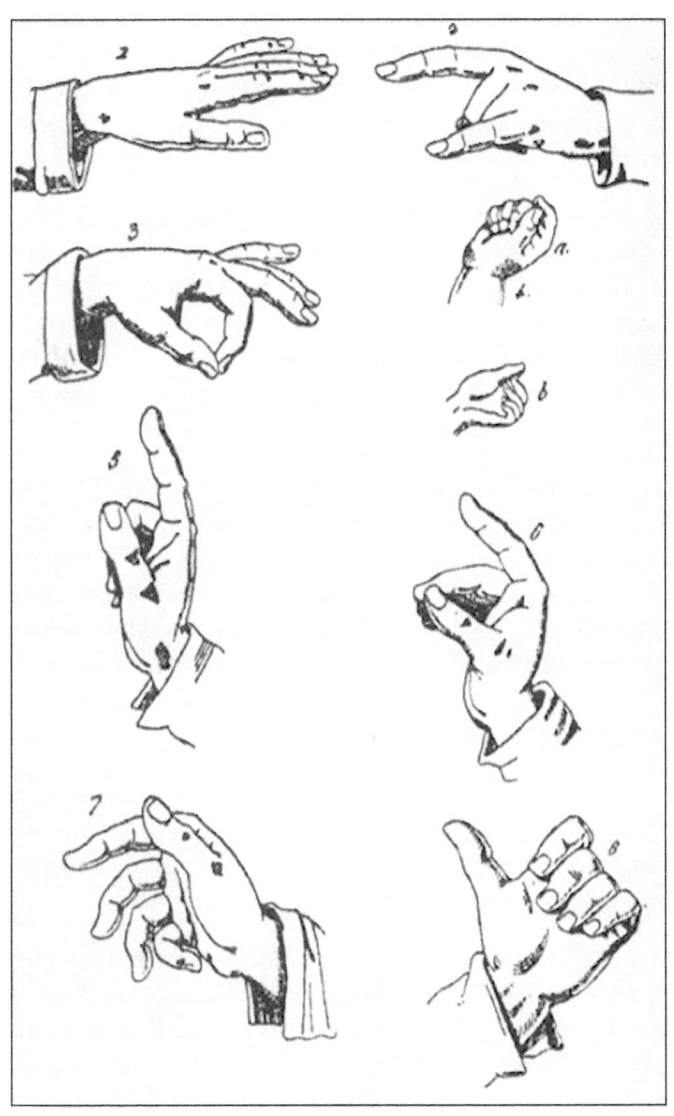

Different hand positions used to ward off the evil eye.

Red amulets are common, and can be worn, carried or placed around the home: red stones and coral, even knots of red yarn (old European customs call for weaving red yarn into clothing and hanging bunches of red yarn from horses' harnesses).

Blue is another color that wards off malevolent staring and the evil eye. In Middle Eastern cultures, round eyes made of cobalt blue glass are worn on the body and placed around homes. In parts of America, such as the Appalachians, the term "haint blue" refers to a shade of blue used to paint rooms, which will ward off ghosts ("haints") and malevolent influences.

However, there is no need to recite incantations, wear amulets or spit if you find yourself the object of a malevolent stare. Break eye contact as quickly as possible and visualize any energetic links as dissolving or shattering. Take a few deep breaths and visualize the golden white light from the Source of All Being circulating throughout the body and extending into the aura, with violet light beneath it as a protective barrier.

In some situations, breaking eye contact may be difficult. Perhaps your malevolent starer is someone you must converse with on a daily basis, such as a co-worker. You can't always avert your vision.

There is, however, an excellent remedy that gives the appearance of maintaining eye contact. Instead of looking into the other person's eyes, fix your gaze on the bridge of the nose just where it meets the forehead. You will give the appearance of eye contact, but the baleful gaze will be averted and flow around you.

The blue eye amulet is hung in windows and on doors to keep negative forces away. It is also fashioned into charms and jewelry.

If you are sitting, you can also break the energy by crossing your feet at the ankles and folding your hands over your abdomen, which protects the sacral chakra.

Another remedy is to visualize a thick piece of plate glass as a barrier between you and the other person. It is like a one-way glass, in that you can continue to see and react to the other, but nothing they are sending out in negative energy can penetrate the glass and reach you.

Chapter 7

Dream and Sleep Invasion

A nightmare is any dream that is unsettling or frightening to the dreamer. The term "nightmare" is based on the Scandinavian word *mara*, which is a nocturnal spirit that torments sleeping people. Nightmares vary from dreams in which we are in unpleasant circumstances to truly terrifying and vivid experiences in which we are threatened, harmed or in great danger. Some persistent nightmares are part of psychological stress syndromes and require therapeutic help. For many dreamers, the occasional nightmare or repeating nightmare deals with unhappy circumstances that need attention in waking life; they cease when the problem is rectified.

There is another kind of nightmare that has paranormal origins. It differs from ordinary dreams in that it is intensely realistic, even if it seems like a dream. Sometimes these nightmares start in sleep and continue after the person awakens.

Dion Fortune observed that disturbed dreams are often the first sign of a psychic attack. The dreamscape may be invaded, such as by a haunting presence in a specific locale, an opportunistic entity that is able to attach to someone, or by invasion via psychic attack. A vulnerable person might be "dream-attacked" by another person who harbors anger and intense dislike against them. Such dream attacks can be deliberate, or may occur without conscious effort, due to intense negative emotions finding pathways in dreamtime.

The Old Hag syndrome

Psychic attack often involves a sleep and dream disturbance known as the Old Hag syndrome. Characteristics of the Old Hag syndrome vary but have a core motif. If you were to have a hag attack, it probably would unfold like this:

> *You are awakened from sleep by the sound of soft footfalls in the dark. Someone – or some thing – is approaching your bed. Your heart pounds and you lie motionless, straining to see into the dark, yet terrified of what might be revealed. You see nothing. The footfalls*

The Nightmare, after Henry Fuseli. A demon presses upon a sleeping woman while a spirit horse looks on.

come closer. They sound like shoes being dragged across velvet. Slowly. Deliberately.

You sense a presence but still see nothing. Your chest aches from your pounding heart. You sweat. The presence takes on a tangible feel. It looms closer, an ink stain barely perceptible in the night. It emanates evil energy. A disgusting smell fills the air.

Suddenly you are pressed into the bed by an enormous weight upon your chest. The air is slammed from your lungs, and the weight is so heavy you can scarcely take in new air. You feel as though you are suffocating. You try to struggle and scream out, but your limbs are paralyzed, and the scream strangles in your throat. You see a shape on top of you, and it isn't human! Two red eyes glare at you. You are wild with fear that this thing is going to kill you, but you are powerless to save yourself or summon help.

Abruptly and without warning, just as you think you are going to pass out or die, the attack ends. The thing with its red eyes vanishes. You draw in great draughts of air. For a long time, you are afraid to move, lest your movements summon the entity to descend upon you once again and finish you off. You feel exhausted.

Nothing happens. The night is still and silent. When you feel confident enough, you turn on a light, rise and inspect the house. Nothing is amiss. You return to bed.

Still shaky, you cannot sleep. You stay awake the rest of the night, on your guard against the return of the thing.

The Old Hag syndrome has been recorded since ancient times. The second-century Roman physician, Galen, wrote about it, and chalked it up to something that happens due to indigestion. Gastric disturbances might indeed cause unsettled dreams, but many an Old Hag victim has been attacked on an empty stomach.

In later centuries, these experiences were termed "Old Hag" because they were associated with witches and demons who were believed to go out at night and "ride" on the chests of their victims.

When a nightmare isn't "just a bad dream"

Elizabeth (a pseudonym) is a woman who has experienced a certain nightmare periodically throughout her life. An invisible but palpable evil presence suddenly makes itself known beside her bed and then sexually molests her. There are no sounds or smells, but the bedroom takes on a heavy, unpleasant atmosphere.

To Elizabeth, the nightmares are not "just bad dreams" but strange and very real experiences that involve dreams. Sometimes she isn't certain whether she is awake or dreaming. The attacks are unpredictable, and she has never been able to link them to anything in particular; however, she acknowledges she carries a lot of internal anger and frustration and has never had a satisfactory sexual relationship. She refers to the invading presence as "It." In the past, she tried to send It away but It always came back.

When Elizabeth's husband died, she was frightened that It would increase its attacks. On its next return, she screamed at It to go away and leave her alone for good. Perhaps her intensity of emotion (righteous anger) made the critical difference, for It left without molesting her and never returned.

A psychologist might regard these dreams as caused by repressed sexual tension and emotions that were relieved by the death of the husband. This explanation never satisfied Elizabeth, who regarded It as an external force that somehow managed to invade her dreams.

She is not alone. Her experiences are another example of the Old Hag syndrome.

Characteristics of the Old Hag

The dominant characteristic of an Old Hag experience is, as noted, an unpleasant entity or presence that invades the room. Sometimes, but not always, it comes up on the bed and may press upon or sexually assault the victim. Other characteristics of hag attacks are awful smells; grunting, shuffling, scraping and unpleasant sounds; grotesque dark shapes which may have red eyes; and a pervasive atmosphere of fear. Victims may feel they are having a lucid dream; may be uncertain whether they are awake or dreaming; or may feel completely awake. They often awaken in the morning feeling drained and exhausted, as in this example:

Dream and Sleep Invasion

From time to time, I have these dreams in which a horrible "something" is trying to get into me to take possession of me. I never see it, but I can "feel" it – I know it is there. I always feel like I'm awake when this happens. I try to make it go away, but just when it seems that it's going to get me, I wake up for real. I am always exhausted all day long after one of these dreams.

Folklorist David J. Hufford researched the most comprehensive study of the Old Hag syndrome. In his book *The Terror That Comes in the Night* (1982), he describes different hag attacks, including this one had by a man, in which the attacking presence was white rather than black:

The first thing that occurred to me was that I was dreaming. When it [the hag] got into the room, it sat down on the floor and it looked to me like an elephant, of all things! Just a blob, but white. I was – ah – I knew I wasn't dreaming! I thought I was dreaming but I knew I wasn't dreaming! And I broke out into a sweat and was just forced onto the bed.

According to Hufford, both males and females of all ages experience the Old Hag. Victims can be sleeping at night or napping during the day. They almost always are sleeping on their backs. The attacks usually end as suddenly as they start, and the entity disappears, leaving the victim terrified. (Note: while Hufford does not rule out possible supernatural causes, he does not conclude the Old Hag is a type of psychic attack. He writes that no single explanation, however, fits the syndrome.)

From my case files is the account of "Sheila," who had a history of haunting and hag dreams from childhood. Sheila said of herself, "I am a really happy, out-going person. I love life and I make a conscious effort every single day to thank God for something that He has shared with me, or the experiences that I have had. I have prayed every night since I was a little girl because I used to hear my grandparents whispering prayers in their room before they went to sleep. I knew it must be important."

The nightmares were hard for her to understand:

> *They have continued into my adult life. They are recurrences. The majority of my nightmares take place in a house. It is a mansion out in the country, very old southern style. I have never seen this house, been to anything like this house, nor do I have I any relatives that have lived in such a house, at least as far as I know. I have a large family. This is my nightmare house.*
>
> *Sometimes the house is grand and beautiful, but most of the time it is almost demolished and overgrown with weeds. It has a horseshoe driveway, and there are more trees and such on the right side of it. It also has a big front yard. It is always haunted and only on a few occasions has someone I've known lived in it. I am always trapped*

in it. Usually, I am either trying to open or close a door, but some force won't let me. It's very cold and I usually get a strange smell. I can't describe it. If fear has a smell, I am sure that would be it. I don't associate it with anything pleasant. When I get it, I know that something bad is going to happen.

All kinds of different things occur in these dreams, but the house and its surroundings are basically the same. This house has been with me for as long as I can remember. I am trying to figure out what it means.

The other dream that I have is similar in nature in that I have had it since I was a child. The first one that I really remember was when I was about eight or nine. I dream that I am lying in bed and I hear someone enter my parent's room and then my brother's room. I hear heavy breathing and get that weird smell that I mentioned before. Suddenly, this man (because that is what I sense) comes into my room. I wake up just as I see the silver blade of a knife coming right down at me. I literally wake up screaming and drenched. You could wring my clothes out.

I didn't remember many of those types of dreams for a few years until I got into my twenties. At one time I was having them about every two to three months. These dreams were always the same. I'd be sleeping, I'd hear someone come into my room, I'd hear breathing, I'd even feel the pressure on *the bed. At this point I'd start telling myself to open my eyes, that it was just a dream, but my eyelids are so heavy that it is nearly impossible. Later in life they did not include the knife aspect. I just awaken with no one there and my heart beating out of control.*

On one weird occasion, I felt a cat-like creature walking on the bed and even felt its whiskers on my nose just before I woke up. I don't have a cat. Only once did I actually get a vision of a man's face as I woke up.

All of these dreams take place in the morning, usually after I kiss my boyfriend goodbye and drift back to sleep. These dreams are so realistic that I feel like I am being haunted. They have occurred in many different places that I have lived.

What is the Old Hag?

No one knows exactly what the Old Hag is, but various dark forces are part of the syndrome. As noted, in earlier centuries the Old Hag was believed to be a witch or a demon. Shadow people attack sleepers in this manner. Another possible source is a thoughtform.

Remedies

Determining the cause of Old Hag attacks is important to devising appropriate remedies. The physical, mental and emotional health history of the victim must be

Dream and Sleep Invasion

considered. If opportunistic entities are involved, they may be repelled by trying various remedies given in this book for establishing boundaries and weakening and banishing unwanted presences.

Here is an example of the use of appeal for spiritual help; the victim prayed to her guardian angel:

> *The first time I remember having this happen to me was when I was five years old. I could not speak or talk; I remember trying to call my mom, but nothing came out. I felt the presence of something with me in the same room. It was hard to breathe, and I was very wide awake. This has happened five or six times in my life so far. The last time this occurred, I felt the presence of something in my room, like I was being watched, so I knew it [the choking presence] was going to happen, so I said my guardian angel prayer and the feeling slowly went away.*

Sometimes the attacks are place-specific – there is a resident hostile entity attached to the land – and relief is obtained by leaving. In other cases, the attacks are related to attachments to a person.

One case described by Hufford involved three college girls who shared a lonely country house. One of them had a history of being a psychic lightning rod: wherever she lived, weird things happened, such as poltergeist and haunting phenomena and Old Hag attacks.

Soon after the girls moved in, the "lightning rod" girl began experiencing nightmares. The nightmares spread like a virus to the other girls, increasing in unpleasantness and violent, bloody imagery. Soon they were all visited by a hag presence. Poltergeist phenomena occurred in the house. They called in a priest to bless the house, but that only made things worse. Finally, they had no recourse but to leave the house, and they went their separate ways.

The two secondarily affected girls experienced relief. Whether or not the "lightning rod" girl continued to have problems in not known.

There are cases on record of Old Hag attacks occurring in overnight establishments – hotels, motels, bed and breakfast inns, and so on. Whatever entity or presence is responsible, it is resident to the land and/or the structure.

Bedroom changes

Sometimes changing the position of a bed will help disrupt negativity and make it difficult for an attack to take place. In some of my cases, I have noticed that the attacking presence acts like it follows an energetic pathway, manifesting first in the same place in a room and then following a line.

The head of a bed should never face north, which is the direction associated with negative forces.

Mirrors, which can serve as entry portals, should be eliminated from bedrooms if possible, especially in situations where bedroom visits and attacks are taking place. If mirrors must remain in a bedroom, they should not be over the head of the bed or across from the foot of the bed. Ideally, a person should not be able to see himself in a mirror while in bed. If there are multiple mirrors in a bedroom, make sure they do not face each other or look into each other from any direction, as this will magnify potential portals.

All mirrors are not automatically spirit world portals, however. Many people have mirror-covered closet doors and other mirrors in bedrooms that cause no paranormal difficulty.

Another remedy is to cast a protective circle of light around a bed. This can be done energetically through ritual and visualization.

Finally, there is a reliable folklore remedy: place iron underneath the bed, at the head of the bed, on windowsills, and at the bedroom threshold. More about iron is discussed in the next chapter on Amulets.

CHAPTER 8

AMULETS

An amulet is an object, inscription, drawing or symbol believed to have the power to protect against bad luck, accidents, illnesses, supernatural attack, the evil eye, malevolent stares, psychic attack and other misfortunes. The term "amulet" is derived either from the Latin *amuletum* or the Old Latin *amoletum* for "means of defense." If you ever carried a rabbit's foot or a four-leaf clover, you've carried an amulet for good luck and protection.

Amulets are universal and are answers to age-old, universal needs: to be healthy and successful, fertile and powerful, and to enjoy good fortune. To ancient peoples, these needs were governed by the gods and spirits, who could be either good or evil.

The earliest amulets were natural objects whose unusual shapes, colors or markings indicated they possessed supernatural properties. These items were worn or placed around homes, buildings and tombs as protective objects.

Some objects were protective by sympathetic association: for example, red stones were associated with blood, the life force and vitality, and black stones were associated with rot and negativity.

Precious and semiprecious stones all are considered to have at least some protective properties. Vegetable and fruits can be amulets, such as garlic, a protection against evil and illness. Peach wood and stones (pits) are ancient amulets in Chinese lore.

As civilizations advanced, natural objects were fashioned into jewelry, symbols, animal and human shapes; some were inscribed with prayers or incantations against misfortune. Certain metals were considered powerful against negative forces: iron, gold, silver and copper. The making of an amulet creates protective power, especially if done ritualistically or during certain times.

The ancient Egyptians, Assyrians, Babylonians, Arabs and Hebrews also placed great importance on amulets. The Egyptians used them everywhere. The frog protected fertility; the ankh (a cross with a looped top) guarded everlasting life and generation; the eye of Horus protected health and warded off negativity; the scarab beetle protected against negative magic and guarded resurrection in the afterlife. Some of the amulets made to guard temples were enormous in size. A stone scarab mounted on a pedestal at the temple at Karnak (now on exhibit at the British Museum in London) is five feet long by three feet wide and weighs two tons.

The Assyrians and Babylonians used cylinder seals embedded with semiprecious and precious stones, each stone having its unique magical properties. The cylinder seals were used to impress writing on wet clay. Animal shapes also served as amulets: the ram protected virility, and the bull protected virility and strength.

To invoke the protection of the dead against evil, the Arabs carried small sacks of dust gathered from tombs. They also wore written spells and prayers.

Early Hebrews wore crescent moons to ward off the evil eye and attached bells to clothing to ward off evil spirits.

Eyes and phallic symbols are nearly universal amulets. The names of gods and God, religious symbols and certain magical words and numbers are also universal amulets. Similarly, sacred verses, texts and holy books have protective power.

Amulets for psychic protection

Stones and crystals

Black stones absorb and repel negative energy. Try obsidian, onyx, jet, black agate, hematite and black tourmaline. You can carry a small pebble of black agate or place several of them around the home or work environment.

Smoky quartz has the reputed property of deflecting negative energy as well. It is best when worn on the body, especially as a pendant that rests at the breastbone, or heart chakra level. You can also carry and place smoky quartz.

Turquoise has protective and healing properties and especially benefits the immune system.

Red stones such as ruby, rubellite, garnet, red jasper and carnelian stimulate the life force and are good for restoring depleted energy.

Clear quartz is an excellent crystal to keep in the home and work environment. It promotes clarity of thought and benefits all the layers of the aura and the chakras.

Iron

Iron is an ancient and universal amulet against evil spirits, the evil eye, bewitchments and psychic attack. According to lore, iron not only repels evil but also drains the powers of evil spirits and people.

In earlier times, iron – even in the form of tools – was placed around homes to ward off negative spirits and energy. Women who had just given birth, and their infants, were considered especially vulnerable, and so iron was placed under the mattress, beneath the bed and over the bed.

Iron horseshoes hung over doorways are another version of this protection. Place the open end down and use only three nails (three represents the Holy Trinity). There's an old English folk tale behind this practice. The story goes that a blacksmith named Dunstan was asked by the Devil to fit him with new horseshoes. Dunstan recognized the Devil and nailed a horseshoe onto his hoof, which sent the Devil into agony. Dunstan chained him. He made the Devil promise never to enter a place that had a horseshoe hung over the door, and then released him. Dunstan (909-988) became Abbot of Glastonbury Abbey, Bishop of Worcester, Bishop of London, and Archbishop of Canterbury. He was canonized St. Dunstan in 1029.

In some cases of ongoing psychic attack, I have recommended that iron railroad spikes be placed on windowsills or near a bed and pounded into the earth at the corners of a home and at opposite sides of the entry doors. Old railroad spikes can be purchased in some occult shops, in salvage yards, and on the internet. Iron nails can also work, but I prefer the size and weight of railroad spikes.

Salt

Since ancient times, salt, a preservative essential to health and life itself, has been associated with purity and is therefore a remedy against evil. Centuries ago, salt was more valuable than gold. Roman soldiers were often paid in salt; hence the phrase that someone is "worth his salt." The word "salary" is derived from "salt."

Sharing a person's salt is symbolic of establishing a deep bond between people. In earlier times, when a new home was occupied, salt was often one of the first things to be brought across the threshold in order to drive away evil influences and establish good energy and luck. A pinch of salt was sprinkled before any job or task to ensure the same.

Early Christians began using salt in christenings and baptisms as purification and protection. Church sites were consecrated with salt and holy water. The Catholic ritual of the benediction of salt and water ensures and protects physical health. Oaths sometimes were taken on salt instead of on the Bible.

Salt is thrown at weddings to preserve marital happiness and also to repel evil spirits who might be intent upon wreaking havoc upon the newlyweds. Salt is placed in coffins as a preservative for the soul after death, and to protect it against assaults by evil spirits.

Salt and salted water, especially blessed, are used to cleanse premises infested by demons and negative forces. Salted water is washed around mirrors, windows and doorways, and sometimes washed over walls, ceilings and floors.

Sprinkling salt in an environment is messy, so salt washes are preferable. Window frames and doorway frames can be treated.

Unrefined salt, sea salt and Himalayan Pink Salt contain trace amounts of iron.

Blessed oil

Blessed oil can be applied throughout an environment for exorcism and cleansing. Apply it around mirrors, windows (frames and glass) and door frames.

Some practitioners use blessed oil to make the sign of the cross where they apply it. The cross can be traced, or the finger or thumb can be used to impress oil at the points of a cross.

Seals and sigils

Seals (also called sigils) are inscribed symbols that carry magical power and express spiritual and occult forces, such as contained in a set of ideas, sacred names of God/gods, angels and spirits, and the numerical essences of planetary energies. The term "sigil" comes from the Latin *sigillum*, which means "seal."

Pendants of the seals of the archangels Gabriel, left, and Michael.

Seals and sigils can be known symbols, such as astrological signs and runes, and can be created on an individual basis. Sigils of spirits, such as angels, can be found in magical textbooks.

Seals and sigils are like shorthand. They can be used to call forth spirits. Like other amulets, they serve as a physical focus for a person to link to a spiritual force. For example, the seal of an angel can evoke all the spiritual properties and associations of that angel.

Seals and sigils also can serve as a focus for meditation and contemplation.

The Benedictine Medal

The Catholic Church strikes medals for every saint, and they are popular pieces worn as jewelry and kept in homes and other places. The official medal of St. Benedict was struck in 1880 to commemorate the 14th centenary anniversary of St. Benedict's birth; it is also called the Jubilee Medal. The Benedictine Medal is a major protection against demonic forces.

One side of the medal has an image of Benedict holding his *Rule* in his left hand and a cross in his right. There is a raven on one side of him and a cup with a snake in it on the other side of him, representing his triumphs over wickedness. Around the medal's outer margin are the words *Eius in obitu nostro praesentia muniamur*, Latin for "May we, at our death, be fortified by His presence."

St. Benedict Medal

The other side of the medal has an equilateral cross. The vertical bar bears the initials CSSML, which stand for *"Crux Sacra Sit Mihi Lux"* ("May the Holy Cross be my light."). The horizontal bar bears the initials NDSMD, which stand for *"Non Draco Sit Mihi Dux"* ("Let not the dragon be my overlord.").

On the interior angles of the cross are the initials CSPB, standing for *"Crux Sancti Patris Benedicti"* ("The Cross of the Holy Father Benedict."). At the top of the cross is either the word *"PAX"* ("Peace") or *"I"* for Christ.

Finally, the medal's margin is inscribed with the initials of Benedict's famous *"Vade retro satana"* ("Step back/Begone Satan"), VRSNSMV, which stands for *"Vade Retro Satana, Nunquam Suade Mihi Vana"* ("Begone Satan, do not suggest to me thy vanities"), and SMQLIVB, which stands for *"Sunt Mala Quae Libas, Ipse Venena Bibas"* ("Evil are the things thou profferest, drink thou thy own poison.").

The actual origins of the medal might be much older. According to the *Catholic Encyclopedia*:

> *It is doubtful when the Medal of St. Benedict originated. During a trial for witchcraft at Natternberg near the Abbey of Metten in Bavaria [a Benedictine monastery established in the 8th century] in the year 1647, the accused women testified that they had no power over Metten, which was under the protection of the cross. Upon investigation, a number of painted crosses, surrounded by the letters which are now*

> *found on Benedictine medals, were found on the walls of the abbey, but their meaning had been forgotten.*
>
> *Finally, in an old manuscript, written in 1415, was found a picture representing St. Benedict holding in one hand a staff which ends in a cross, and a scroll in the other. On the staff and scroll were written in full the words of which the mysterious letters were the initials. Medals bearing the image of St. Benedict, a cross, and these letters began now to be struck in Germany, and soon spread over Europe. They were first approved by Benedict XIV in his briefs of 23 December 1741, and 12 March 1742.*

You can see how this one small medal, full of injunctions against the Devil, packs a lot of punch. The Benedictine Medal is worn as jewelry, attached to rosaries, kept in pockets, hung on walls, and even embedded in the foundations of homes and businesses as a literal prayer of exorcism against Satan, and for strength in time of temptation. They are placed over thresholds and beds as amulets.

The medals are mounted at the crossbar of crucifixes that are favored by some demonologists and exorcists.

Miracles have been associated with the medal. For example, Pope Leo IX (r. 1049-1054) was bitten by a snake and credited his miraculous recovery to the medal. Other miracles of healing, including emotional disorders and alcoholism, have been recorded in the literature.

Priests and deacons can bless Benedictine Medals. In the blessing that follows, the priest or deacon recites the versicles and others present give the responses. The sign of the cross is made with the right hand across the body where the + appears:

Versicle. Our help is in the name of the Lord.

Response. Who made heaven and earth.

Versicle. In the name of God the Father + almighty, who made heaven and earth, the seas and all that is in them, I exorcise these medals against the power and attacks of the evil one. May all who use these medals devoutly be blessed with health of soul and body. In the name of the Father + almighty, of the Son + Jesus Christ our Lord, and of the Holy + Spirit the Paraclete, and in the love of the same Lord Jesus Christ who will come on the last day to judge the living and the dead, and the world by fire.

Response. Amen.

Versicle. Let us pray. Almighty God, the boundless source of all good things, we humbly ask that, through the intercession of Saint Benedict, you pour out your blessings + upon these medals. May those who use them devoutly and earnestly strive to perform good works, be blessed by you with health of soul and body, the grace of a holy life, and remission of the temporal punishment due to sin.

May they also with the help of your merciful love, resist the temptation of the evil one and strive to exercise true charity and justice toward all, so that one day they may appear sinless and holy in your sight. This we ask through Christ our Lord.

Response. Amen.

(The medals are then sprinkled with holy water.)

Choosing appropriate personal amulets

You should consider other amulets that, because of their long histories and widespread uses, make them effective in many situations. The kinds of amulets you employ will depend on individual circumstances.

The most important consideration in choosing an amulet is your energetic link to what it represents. The true effectiveness of an amulet is its connection to a spiritual source and power that resonates through your body and being. Choose according to your beliefs.

It doesn't hurt to use other amulets as well. Many of them have long histories going back to ancient times, and thus they have built up a powerful collective thoughtform energy that you can tap into. Again, however, you should

Sacred symbols are among the most frequently used amulets.

have a personal and emotional connection to them and what they represent.

For years, I have worn a Christian cross. When I do casework, and when I lecture, I wear an angel medallion, the seal of the archangel Uriel. I chose Uriel because this angel holds the solar flame of truth – absolute truth – which is a force, along with the light of the Godhead and unconditional love – that vanquishes negativity. I also wear the seal of the archangel Michael, who represents strength, perseverance and the ability to overcome and vanquish negativity and evil. Uriel has a truth energy and Michael has a warrior energy.

Choose amulets according to those that attract you. Pick up and hold physical objects, and if you feel a spark or vibration of energy, that object is speaking to you.

A pendant of the seal of the archangel Uriel.

How to clear and charge amulets

Amulets work the best when you charge them yourself with your own personal power. A charging is like a battery; it eventually runs down, and then a recharging is necessary.

After acquiring an amulet, clear it of existing energies, which could conflict with your own purposes. For example, stones purchased from a shop may have been handled by an unknown number of people, all of whom could have left energy residues.

One of the most common ways of clearing is to let an object rest in salt for a three days. This is not feasible or desirable for all objects because of the corrosive effect of salt, and so instead let the amulet sit in sunlight for three days. Some people use both salt and sunlight for clearing.

If feasible, objects can also be cleared by dipping them into water, especially if you have "magnetized" the water by holding the vessel it is in and projecting purity into it with your thought/intention.

Another way to clear objects is with your own energy. This works best if you are accustomed to meditating and bringing golden white spiritual light into the body. Visualize that light flowing down the arms into the hands and fingers, and out into etheric space. Hold the object in your right hand, and use the left hand, open and palm down, to make passes over the object, going right to left. As you move your hand off to the left, visualize that all unwanted energy is released and moves off into space.

Whatever clearing method you choose, concentrate on all unwanted residues and attachments being removed or dissolved.

After the amulet has been cleared – you should be able to sense this energetically – then charge it with intention. A good general intention is "This_____(object) shall protect me/my home/workplace against all unwanted negative and hostile energy, forces and presences."

Amulets

Objects can also be charged with specific intentions, such as protection against known hostile people or spirits. I prefer general charging, because it is not limiting to factors that may not be known at any given time.

To charge the amulet, cup it in both hands with the right hand on top and visualize the life force light pouring through you and into it while you state, either mentally or out loud, its protective purpose.

Periodically check your amulets for their energy levels. If you sense that they need recharging, follow the steps again. Amulets that absorb negativity, such as black stones, may need to be cleared before recharging.

Chapter 9

More Remedial Measures

Candle burning

Candles have a long and interesting history in religious worship, magic and folklore. They light the way to the sacred; dispel the forces of darkness; are associated with ghosts and the dead; can find buried treasure; and play a role in dreams and visions of the spirit realms.

The origin of candles is not known, but there is evidence that beeswax candles were used in Egypt and Crete as early as 3000 BCE. Other early candles consisted of tapers made of a fibrous material, such as rushes saturated with tallow.

Ancient peoples observed that candle flames revealed mysterious things. By staring into a flame, one could enter an altered state of consciousness and see gods and spirits or the future. The Egyptians of about the 3rd century used lamps, and possibly candles, in a magic ritual for "dreaming true," or obtaining answers from dreams. The individual retired to a dark cave or place facing south and sat and stared into a flame until he saw a god. He then lay down and went to sleep, anticipating that the god would appear in his dreams with the answers he sought.

Candles and lamps were used in religious observances. By the 4th century, both candles and lamps were part of Christian rituals, but it was not until the latter part of the Middle Ages, from the 12th century on, that candles were placed on church altars. The Catholic Church established the use of consecrated holy candles in rituals of blessings and absolving sins, and in exorcizing demons.

To cleanse an environment, burn a black candle all the way down; black absorbs negativity. Then burn a white candle all the way down. White establishes spiritual energy, spiritual truth and strength, purity and purification, and the attraction of benevolent spiritual forces.

If you know you are dealing with jealousy or envy, pair the black candle with a dark green one for jealousy and a yellow one for envy. What is the difference between jealousy and envy? Jealousy is fear of losing something, especially to a rival, and is a factor in love triangles. Envy is the coveting of something you do not have, but someone else does.

More Remedial Measures

If you know you are dealing with hatred or animosity, pair the black candle with a red one. Burn them all the way down, followed by burning a white candle all the way down.

To cleanse each room in a house with candles, light a white candle and walk the boundaries of each room along the walls. Then crisscross the room in an X. Do the same for the ceiling, by holding the candle up in the air. While walking, invoke the cleansing help of angels, the divine, or other spiritual help.

Colored candles can be burned to enhance the environment in different ways and bolster depleted energies, which may be beneficial after a cleansing:

Pink: Love and friendship; harmony; entertaining; morality; domestic tranquility

Red: Sexuality; strength; physical health and vigor; passion; protection

Orange: Courage; communication; solving of legal problems; concentration; encouragement

Yellow: Persuasion; confidence and charm; aid to memory and studying

Green: Healing; money and prosperity; luck; fertility

Blue: Psychic and spiritual awareness; peace; prophetic dreams; protection during sleep

Purple: Ambition; ruling authority; reversing a curse; speeding healing in illness; extra power

Gold: Protection; enlightenment; masculine principle

Silver: Intuition; subconscious; feminine principle

Brown: Protecting pets; solving household problems; attracting help in financial crises

Gray: Stalemate; neutrality; cancellation

For invoking the presence of the four major archangels, use candles of the following colors:

Michael – gold and yellow

Gabriel – white and silver

Raphael – green and orange

Uriel – ice white and ice blue

Scents

Scents have been used for centuries to purify environments and expel unwanted presences. The incense burned in religious services serves this function.

Frankincense and myrrh are good for repelling and cleansing. Smudging with sage is a traditional Native American remedy. Sai flora flaxo is a stronger incense (and quite unpleasant, by the way – it is likely to repel people along with any spirits).

In cases where strong negative entities are lodged in places, scents alone are not likely to be enough to expel them. However, they are essential to restore balance and harmony once a place has been cleared.

Sage smudging traditionally is done with a large abalone shell and a feather. Place the burning sage in the shell and fan the smoke about the environment with the feather. Smudge sticks, which are thick bundles of tied sage, also are used and waved about the air to disperse the smoke.

While saturating an environment with incense or sage, invoke spiritual help to expel unwanted presences and restore balance. Reclaim the sovereignty of your space.

Washes

There are many recipes for washes in folk magic texts. Blessed salt in vinegar is a good wash for thresholds, windowsills and mirror edges. Water with lemon is another natural cleansing agent. Some washes are applied to floors;

make sure your flooring will not be damaged by any wash ingredients. Invoke spiritual help as you spread the wash.

Diet and clothing

Fortune recommended that people under psychic attack add iron-rich red meat to their diet, which is grounding. A vegetarian diet should be avoided.

In extreme cases, she recommended a change of wardrobe, though I have never found that measure to be necessary. In some cases, people have discarded the clothing they were wearing when they believed they picked up an attachment, such as during a paranormal investigation.

Conclusion

Psychic protection is about both prevention and remedy. As I mentioned early on, we all have a natural barrier around us. If you put even a modest effort into taking care of that barrier and strengthening it, you will seldom have a problem with negativity. In the event that a breach occurs, you will be in a stronger position to deal with it, and remedial measures can be taken. Follow the advice in this guide and put into practice the most universal and frequently used measures for building defenses and using remedies.

APPENDIX

A HOME BLESSING

This is a simple ritual for maintaining a harmonious energy balance in your home.

Places absorb energy and reflect that energy back to occupants and visitors. A home should reflect rest, regeneration, peacefulness and harmony – your refuge from the world and sanctuary for your well-being.

Home blessings are simple ceremonies that can be done periodically. You clean your home physically by vacuuming, dusting and straightening things. A home blessing is an energy cleaning. It makes your place sparkle with an inviting warmth.

Home blessings should be done in new homes after you've moved in and settled your belongings. Home blessings should be done in existing homes every few months to keep the energy fresh. I recommend home blessings that coincide with the changing of the seasons: the equinoxes, or March 21-22 and September 21-22, and the solstices, or June 21-22 and December 21-22. Home blessings also can be done whenever there is a major change, such as a renovation, a birth or a death, or a turning point.

Here's how you can do your own home blessings. You can adapt this formula to suit your own needs. To be effective, a ceremony or ritual should come alive with your own creativity.

Start by collecting items that represent the four elements: a small dish of water; a stone, crystal or dish of salt for earth; a feather or incense for air; and a candle for fire. Place them on a cloth-covered tabletop that will serve as your altar. You can add anything else that feels appropriate, such as a small plant or personal and religious items. Set up an altar in the living room, which is the main room that is fed by all other rooms.

Light your candle (and incense, if you've chosen that) and open your ceremony with a prayer that gives thanks for the home itself. Mention all the things you like and appreciate about it. The prayer can be spontaneous, or something you've composed in advance for reading. Mention any special purposes, such as new home, change of season or transitions.

Appendix

Take the candle and walk from room to room. In every room, say a short prayer; for example, "I ask for the blessings of love and protection in this room for family, friends and guests." Or name a person if the room is theirs.

When you are done making a circuit of the house, return to the living room. Place your candle back on the altar. End with a closing prayer; for example, "I/We give thanks for the sanctuary of this beautiful home. May the love here continue to grow, nourish us and bless us."

The occultist Franz Bardon advised that it is essential to charge or "load" one's living space with vital force and intention:

> *With the help of your vital force, charge a room with the desire that you feel well in it. Enthrall this force with the desire that, as long as you live in the room, the influence should persist, continue renewing, and keep doing so, even when you leave the room and are absent for some time. Should anyone else enter your room ignoring that there is an accumulation of vital force, he will feel very uncomfortable in your dwelling. Now and again, you can reinforce the density and power of your radiant energy in your room by repeating the desire. If you live in a room influenced in such a favorable way, the stored vital force will always exert a good influence on your health, and consequently on your body.*

If you love your home, your home will love you back and protect you as well. Like a mirror, it will reflect the emotions you offer it.

Here is an Omaha Native American prayer for the home:

> May the house wherein I dwell be blessed;
> May good thoughts here possess me;
> May my path of life be straight and true;
> My dreams as here I lie be joyous;
> All above, below, about me
> May the house I love be hallowed.

About the Author

Rosemary Ellen Guiley is an author, researcher and investigator in the paranormal and body-mind-spirit fields. She has written more than 65 books on a broad range of topics, including how to develop your psychic power. Rosemary's years of experience dealing with cases of problem hauntings, negative spirits and entities, and psychic attack and vampirism required the development of effective protection measures. She has studied energy healing, occult and folk remedies, and other measures of protection and banishment.

Some of her works pertaining to this book are *The Encyclopedia of Vampires and Werewolves*, *The Encyclopedia of Magic and Alchemy, The Encyclopedia of Demons & Demonology, Guide to the Dark Side of the Paranormal* and *Guide to Psychic Power.*

Rosemary is founder and president of Visionary Living Publishing, a division of Visionary Living, Inc., her media and publishing enterprise. She is Executive Editor of FATE magazine.

Websites: **www.visionaryliving.com** and **www.visionarylivingpublishing.com**

Further Reading

Bardon Franz. *Initiation into Hermetics: A Course of Instruction of Magic Theory and Practice.* Holladay, UT: Merkur Publishing, 2016. *[Note: a good text for those seeking advanced training.]*

Evans, Darren and Rosemary Ellen Guiley. *The Zozo Phenomenon.* New Milford, CT: Visionary Living, Inc., 2016.

Elworthy, Frederick Thomas. *The Evil Eye: The Classic Account of an Ancient Superstition.* New York: Dover Publications, 2004.

Fortune, Dion. *Psychic Self-Defense: The Classic Instruction Manual for Protecting Yourself Against Paranormal Attack.* Revised edition. Newburyport, MA: Red Wheel Weiser, 2011.

Guiley, Rosemary Ellen with Rick Fisher. *Ouija Gone Wild: Shocking True Stories.* New Milford, CT: Visionary Living, Inc., 2012.

Guiley, Rosemary Ellen. *Guide to the Dark Side of the Paranormal.* New Milford, CT: Visionary Living, Inc., 2012.

_____. *The Djinn Connection: The Hidden Links Between Djinn, Shadow People, ETs, Nephilim, Archons, Reptilians & Other Entities.* New Milford, CT: Visionary Living, Inc., 2013.

_____. *Calling Upon Angels: How Angels Help Us in Daily Life.* New Milford, CT: Visionary Living, Inc., 2015.

_____. *Guide to Psychic Power.* New Milford, CT: Visionary Living, Inc., 2015.

Hufford, David J. *The Terror That Comes in the Night: An Experience-Centered Study of Supernatural Assault Traditions.* Philadelphia: University of Pennsylvania Press, 1982.

Phillips, Melita and Osborne Denning. *Practical Guide to Psychic Self-Defense and Well-Being.* Woodbury, MN: Llewellyn Worldwide, 1989.

Further Reading

Ravensdale, Tom and James Morgan. *The Psychology of Witchcraft.: An Account of Witchcraft, Black Magic, and the Occult.* New York: J. Bartholomew, 1974.

Zaffis, John and Rosemary Ellen Guiley. *Haunted by the Things You Love.* New Milford, CT: Visionary Living, Inc., 2014.

Don't stop now! Improve your spiritual strength even more with Rosemary Ellen Guiley's *Guide to Psychic Power*, an excellent companion to this book.

Guide to Psychic Power is a self-study handbook packed with proven exercises that will help you:

- Boost your aura strength
- Improve your meditation
- Increase your natural intuitive/psychic ability
- Use your power to make better decisions
- Enhance your well-being
- And much more

Get your copy of *Guide to Psychic Power* in print on Amazon and at select retailers, and in ebook on Kindle, Apple, Nook, Kobo and Google Play.

www.ingramcontent.com/pod-product-compliance
Lightning Source LLC
Chambersburg PA
CBHW021152080526
44588CB00008B/305